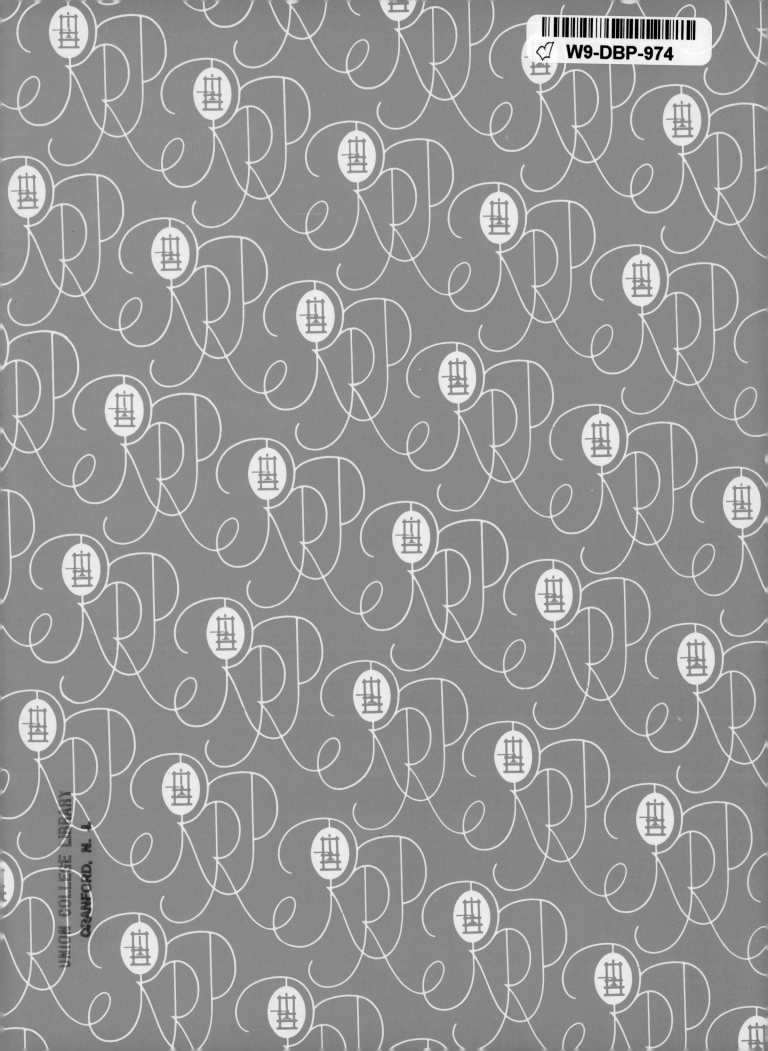

The Theatre Student

COMPLETE PRODUCTION GUIDE

TO MODERN MUSICAL THEATRE

 # THE THEATRE STUDENT SERIES

Robert R. Buseick directed the musical version of Peter Pan, *produced by Beaverton High School, Beaverton, Oregon. The production involved more than 100 students who, besides acting and playing in the orchestra, built the sets, made the costumes, and planned every detail, even including the intricate flying system. This production is typical of the thousands of outstanding musicals being produced by high schools, colleges, and little theatre groups each year.*

The Theatre Student

COMPLETE PRODUCTION GUIDE TO MODERN MUSICAL THEATRE

Tom Tumbusch

with drawings by David Shurte

PUBLISHED BY
RICHARDS ROSEN PRESS, INC.
NEW YORK, N.Y. 10010

Standard Book Number: 8239–0149–1

Library of Congress Catalog Card Number: 79–75380
Dewey Decimal Classification: 792

Published in 1969 by Richards Rosen Press, Inc.
29 East 21st Street, New York City, N.Y. 10010

First Edition

Manufactured in the United States of America

CONTENTS

To my Father and Mother, who provided the discipline and creative freedom that made this book possible.

ABOUT THE AUTHOR

TOM TUMBUSCH first became seriously interested in the musical theatre during his college years at the University of Dayton, when he appeared in productions of *Finian's Rainbow, The Boy Friend,* and *Guys and Dolls.* After graduation in 1962, he remained at the university as choreographer for *Little Mary Sunshine* (the first production in which many of the ideas presented in this book were tested), *The Fantasticks,* and *Wonderful Town.*

While still an undergraduate, he began to think about writing a book on musical theatre and initiated serious research on the subject. His research was entirely original and from primary sources, such as the opening-week *Playbills* of many shows and nearly complete collections of souvenir programs, *Theatre Arts* magazine, scripts, newspaper reviews, and original-cast record albums. An avid fan of the nuts and bolts behind musical production, he has had the opportunity to observe many Broadway musicals in the making. In addition, much of the material in the book is drawn from his own work.

He is the author of numerous articles on the musical theatre in such publications as *Dramatics* magazine and *Musical Show,* and he is performing arts editor of *Dayton USA,* the Chamber of Commerce publication, and Dayton correspondent for *Variety.*

With all this, however, the musical theatre is an avocation for Tom Tumbusch —he makes his living as account executive for Yeck and Yeck Advertising in Dayton.

PREFACE

As far as I can determine, this is the first step-by-step production guide to modern musical theatre. It is based on the premise that a musical production is vastly different from that of a straight play, both in its philosophy of creativity and method of presentation. Also, that a play is mounted *into* a production whereas the production is actually *part of* a musical.

With the bigness of musical production comes the larger cast and production crew, the orchestra, detailed preplanning, a new approach to sets and set changes, plus new problems of coordination.

Whereas a play has but one director, a musical usually has three sources of creativity—the stage director, the choreographer, and the musical director. Whenever there is more than one creative source, artistic differences are bound to occur. The problem can be further compounded by the people responsible for sets and costumes, who also have some say on how the production will be put together. Yet it is vital that the whole production staff act as one unified force, having resolved all differences prior to rehearsals.

Musicals pose new and more complex problems. Solutions that worked for play productions are no longer valid, since a musical is more than just a play with music and dancing.

The purpose of this book is to provide a new understanding of what a musical is and how it should be presented. Following the Introduction and the first two chapters, which provide help in the all-important task of selecting the *best* musical *for your group,* a system for organizing a musical production is presented. As they say in *Bells Are Ringing,* it's a "simple little system"—a step-by-step procedure requiring nothing more than a script and a sincere desire to produce an outstanding production to put into practice. If it appears to be a little more work at first reading, try it! See how it saves time where it counts, in those last weeks of rehearsal. It goes a long way to solve communications problems and, if followed, practically guarantees a better musical production.

The last seven chapters on the individual production functions (Director, Choreographer, Settings, etc.) serve two purposes: 1) helpful hints to the person(s) performing the particular function and 2) a synopsis for other members of the production staff that they may better understand the jobs of people with whom they must coordinate. The *bigness* of musical productions dictates a more professional treatment of these old—yet new—problems.

Besides my own knowledge and research, this book benefits from the experience of more than 150 high schools, colleges, and community theatre organizations that were kind enough to reply to my national Musical Comedy Production Questionnaire. Reference to this survey appears throughout the text. A complete summary will be found on page 171.

As much as possible, I have tried to deal with specific problems inherent in modern musical theatre production and to avoid a rehash of basic stagecraft.

This book comes at a time when the number of nonprofessional groups producing local revival productions of Broadway musical comedies is rising at a phenomenal rate each year. Although there are enough books on play production and related fields to fill a small library, the complexities that arise with the words "musical theatre" have, in my opinion, never been practically presented in any single volume. I hope you will find *Complete Production Guide to Modern Musical Theatre* the first.

Like any book or any musical production, this one took a major team effort. The cooperation I enjoyed from schools and theatre groups filling out questionnaires and submitting photographs was beyond my greatest expectations.

I am particularly indebted to three dedicated and knowledgeable individuals—Patrick Gilvary, Director of the University of Dayton Players, and Bob Buseick, Dramatic Director of Beaverton (Oregon) High School, for their help and suggestions on the entire manuscript; and especially to Larry Tagg, Associate Professor of Music, University of Dayton, for his patient and understanding help in preparing the chapter on Musical Direction. Also, a note of special thanks to Jack Nakano of Youth Theatre Productions and Santa Barbara High School, who contributed many useful suggestions.

For help on the drawings, my thanks to Dave Shurte. And finally my deep appreciation to my secretarial staff, Betty Traylor, Jay Machler, and in particular my wife Marty, who shared her courtship and early marriage with the writing of this book.

Tom Tumbusch
Dayton, Ohio

FOREWORD

Several years ago, while in the early stages of rehearsal for a musical—I think it was *Little Mary Sunshine*—I noticed that one of the leads was somewhat at a loss as to what everybody else was writing down in their sides during the blocking. He was new to the group but had had several years of experience in high-school and community musical productions, so I kept an eye on him and hoped that whatever the problem was, it would work itself out. Finally he could stand the confusion no longer, and he asked me, "What do you mean by blocking? What is it? How do I go about it?" Admittedly I should have told him when we started, but knowing of his previous experience I had taken for granted that he knew some form of "blocking." I, of course, immediately explained the process and then asked him what he had done in his previous roles. His answer: "Oh, we did whatever we wanted to, and when the number was over we just took a bow and moved offstage." Mind you, he was not talking about variety shows, but about high-school and community productions of Broadway hits such as *Guys and Dolls*.

This revelation, coupled with frantic calls to my office from local producing organizations trying to make some sense out of chaos one or two days before opening a musical, can lead only to the conclusion that some definitive guidelines are needed. The producer, whether it be a high-school literature or music teacher or just an ambitious theatre buff, may have all the ambition, spirit, and energy in the world, but the lack of practical know-how and technical organization can destroy him. Theatre cannot afford to lose the people of fortitude with or without the necessary background to produce a show.

Musical productions offer the greatest opportunities for the greatest number of people. Inherent in these opportunities are the problems, potential or actual. There are libraries of books on theory and form but Mr. Tumbusch has taken the production apart and then piece by painstaking piece he has reassembled and coordinated all of its multifaceted aspects. To the best of my knowledge, there is not a book in any library that has this much-needed approach.

Mr. Tumbusch's ideas have been tried and tested in the heat of battle. They work. If there is one all-encompassing, pragmatic hosanna in theatre production, it is just that. IT WORKS!

PATRICK S. GILVARY
DIRECTOR, UNIVERSITY OF
DAYTON PLAYERS

LIST OF FIGURES AND ILLUSTRATIONS

INTRODUCTION

*"Dim the House Lights;
Cue the Conductor"*

For the past twenty or more years, crepe-hanging critics have lamented over the dying American Theatre. Maybe such thinking is an extension of the old "movies-killed-vaudeville" logic or perhaps it is based on any number of other statistics. Certainly theatre has suffered from television, higher-priced tickets and production costs, loss of younger audiences, and competition from the eternally growing number of other entertainment outlets. Professional theatre is also bogged down in a sticky sea of tradition and monopolistic controls. Its interdependency on the established producers, theatre owners, and theatrical suppliers make it practically impossible for independent outside companies or producers to get a foothold.

THEATRE GAINS NEW MOMENTUM

Yet there are many reasons why theatre will always survive. Broadway is finally taking steps to unravel the aging ties that are threatening to choke out its very existence. The special December, 1964, edition of *Playbill* placed a surprising number of inside theatrical facts before the public for the first time. In that issue detailed data on production costs and other problems were aired by leading theatrical personalities. Many stirring changes were proposed and several have since been put into practice. Government aid to the performing arts, enacted in 1966, promises more long-range improvements over the theatre of earlier times.

Broadway is growing. The first new theatre in thirty years, the New York State Theater at Lincoln Center, has been established as a sanctuary of American musical theatre, presenting revival productions of American musical classics and encouraging new works. Farther downtown, in the heart of the theatre district, other activities give life to the resurging theatre. Theatres are being remodeled and converted back from TV studios. The Mark Hellinger, St. James, Helen Hayes, Broadhurst, Lunt-Fontanne and Majestic have been ex-

tensively remodeled. (All but the Helen Hayes house musical productions.) The Broadway Theatre at 53rd Street has been reconverted from a television studio, and the famous Palace, long a movie house, has once more been restored to legitimate production. (Both present musical productions.)

The average number of productions per season is a far cry from the all-time peak of 278 new shows produced in the 1927–28 season, but modern-day hit shows run much longer than those of yesteryear. Many of the older productions were scarcely more than variety shows, in any case. Writing styles have changed. Newer theatres are larger. New forms of entertainment are with us. Production costs are way up.

Considering these factors, the alleged problem with Broadway is really only one of numbers. Today's long-run shows have replaced a larger number of short-run ventures similar to the variety hours and "specials" now seen on TV. With the advent of higher standards, the total number of new productions has dropped, but the percentage of shows achieving a respectable run has actually increased.

Outside New York City, theatrical growth has been even more spectacular. Other areas of professional theatrical growth have been summer stock companies (several performing all year round), repertory theatres, and a rising number of new "road" theatres. Commenting on the building of the $162,000,000 Lincoln Center for the Performing Arts, *Business Week* (Jan. 29, 1966) said, "The eight-year Lincoln Center experience is looked to as a guide by 35 other U.S. communities now building or planning performing arts centers, and by the builders of some 70 other civic centers that make some provision for the performing arts." *

After many years of stagnation, the "road" is once more coming alive. New legitimate theatres in the West, joined by sparkling replacement theatres in Toronto, Detroit, Baltimore, and other cities, are leading the way to year-round decentralized legitimate theatre. During the 1966–67 season traveling road shows, paced by the musicals, *Hello, Dolly!* and *Fiddler on the Roof,* grossed over $42,-000,000 to set an all-time record. Never before have so many different people in so many different cities seen top stars in top shows.

As for nonprofessional theatre, a study entitled *The Performing Arts–Problems and Prospects,* sponsored by the Rockefeller Foundation, reports: "The community and amateur theatre movement in the United States has assumed large proportions. In 1964, there were approximately five thousand formal amateur theatre groups having some continuity of organization, while other groups, performing on varied schedules, were estimated at about thirty-five thousand. Performances vary enormously in quality, but some are good enough to compete vigorously with professional theatre.

"All this activity demonstrates the broad appeal of the theatre in this country. It is a well-loved art form, and one that may have the best possibility of quickly developing wide, new support, cutting across all social and cultural lines." *

THE ROLE OF THE MUSICAL

There are probably many reasons for the current heights of theatrical activity, but one of the most important is the modern musical comedy. Many people prefer the term "musical" because the production form can be a comedy, drama, mystery, or other entertainment. The term "musical comedy" still carries a connotation of early 20th-century George M. Cohan, Ziegfeld Follies, or George White's Scandals sort of production. However, throughout this book the terms "musical" or "musical comedy" or "musical theatre" will be used indiscriminately and will mean the integrated book-music-lyric musical shows predominant since the overwhelming success of *Oklahoma!* in 1943.

Wherever theatre is growing, with the possible exception of the repertory theatre movement, a big factor is the growth and acceptance of musical productions. On Broadway the greatest percentage of successful shows are musicals. In a season of 60 legitimate productions there will be approximately 15 musicals. It is

a rare season when more than 10 percent of the new plays are carried into the next, while it is not at all uncommon to find better than 50 percent of the musical productions lasting for at least one full season or more. There is also greater potential for a Broadway musical to continue its run on the road.

Musicals are the main attraction on the road. Not only have they figured heavily in the resurgence of new legitimate theatres, but also in year-round schedules of live theatrical entertainment. One example is the Fisher Theatre in Detroit. In its first five years (since 1961), this fantastically beautiful theatre (which boasts the largest series subscription advance sale in the professional theatre) played a ratio of better than two musicals to every play. The five-year totals included 43 book musicals, 21 plays or repertory groups, and 12 musical revues or one-man shows.

The summer stock movement cut its teeth and grew strong on the musical comedy. The straw-hat circuit was around for many years, but when large musical comedies permitted hiring of big-name stars the business skyrocketed a hundredfold in less than ten years.

Many summer stock companies present nothing but musicals. A great many carry the term "musical" as part of their name. But by and large most professional summer theatres still present a mixed slate of musicals and plays. In virtually every case known to the author, the musicals outnumber the plays two or three to one.

It is difficult to define the full impact of the musical produced by nonprofessional groups.

An article that appeared Jan. 31, 1965, on the front page of the Sunday *New York Times* business section (of all places) related: "Because of the proliferation of stock, community, college, and school theatrical organizations, the sale of rights to perform musicals and straight plays is currently at a peak. Today the business runs into seven figures.

"More than 100,000 nonprofessional troupes put on a half-million plays and musicals annually, seen by some 100 million persons." *

That news story was published at a given point on a continuing growing trend of nonprofessional theatrical production. There are no signs that such a growth trend has weakened and many reasons to believe that the upward trend has become more acute, especially in the area of musical theatre productions.

In the Rockefeller study on the performing arts, published later in 1965: "Elmer Rice has

SWAYZE STUDIO

Carousel, *Hill Country Arts Foundation, Ingram, Texas, William Y. Hardy, director.*

estimated that the annual attendance at amateur theatrical performances is fifty million, which he believed to be probably ten times the attendance at professional performances." The difference between the *Times's* and the Rockefeller study group's estimates points up how sketchy the boundaries of this vast field really are. If the real figure was a compromise midway between these two estimates, the 75,000,000-member audience would be fifteen times that of professional theatregoers. The author estimates that 33 percent, or 25,000,000, are musical theatre audiences and by the time the total real figure reaches a 100,000,000 combined audience, the proportionate audience for musicals will surpass 50 percent, or a 50,000,000 share of total nonprofessional audiences.

The musical is also on the rise in allied fields. The number of musical comedy specials on television—either special videotaped productions or airing of movie versions—has grown tremendously. And during 1967 no

fewer than sixteen film musicals budgeted for over $80,000,000 (Broadway musicals or originals such as *Doctor Doolittle* and *Star!*) were announced by major Hollywood movie studios —one film musical, *Finian's Rainbow,* having had its Broadway premiere back in 1947.

In building a case for the musical, great care must be taken not to overshadow the merits of straight play production. Much as the author is a proponent of musical productions, it would be foolhardy to suggest that any well-rounded theatre or school group do musicals exclusively. Some light opera companies and musical groups do nothing but musical comedy and operettas. But that is their purpose and, thanks to their specializing, their productions are usually much better than the average musical production. But for any kind of educational institution or any group representing the sole theatrical exposure within a reasonably large area must, as a responsibility to both group members and audiences, provide a well-rounded program of musicals and plays.

The King and I, *Leuzinger High School, Lawndale, California, Julian R. Hughes, director.*

NONPROFESSIONAL MUSICAL THEATRE—
FROM THE BEGINNING

Producing a musical comedy is not a new idea. D. F. Barreca, then director of the Astoria Community Theatre, contributed the following to a contest conducted by The Billboard Publishing Company back in 1924:

The committee felt that no more than $20 could be spent for an entertainment and I, therefore, started in with the intention of producing a George M. Cohan entertainment for one hour with the magnificent sum of $20. The first step was to secure suitable talent and after three days I found that we had practically none. Three or four people could sing, a few more could dance, another could recite and another modestly admitted that he was good at telling jokes. A play was evidently out of the question, and feeling that no one has ever sat thru an amateur minstrel that could possibly help it

I tried to purchase a musical comedy, and found to my surprise that I could not buy one. One gentleman offered to write one for $50, but his offer was quickly rejected. (*The Billboard's Little Theatre Handbook,* published by The Billboard Publishing Company, New York, N.Y. 1924.)

The big advantage modern groups have over this early would-be musical producer is the easy availability of even the latest Broadway hits. The budget would need to be many times $20, but that was extremely low, even for 1924. The talent picture, on the other hand, may seem unchanged. In some areas talent may be in short supply, but in most there is an abundance. As more high schools get into the act, the picture will brighten all the way along the line.

As for the gentleman who was willing to write a musical for $50? Certainly such initiative is not to be discouraged. If any capable person can write a musical comedy suitable for paid admissions, $50 is not at all an unreasonable price to pay just for the typing and manuscript paper he would need to do the job properly.

Availability started to increase in the 1930's when America turned to entertainment to help bind up the depression wounds. The early nonprofessional musical productions were the turn-of-the-century operettas and comic operas in the style of Gilbert and Sullivan. During the 1940's musical comedy completed the transition from revue style to a musical story style that started in the early 1920's and took giant steps with such productions as *Showboat, On Your Toes, Pal Joey,* and, finally, *Oklahoma!*

After World War II, demand for amateur rights to the Rodgers and Hammerstein powerhouses, plus the increase in theatrical interest on the part of returning servicemen with USO experience, started the ball rolling for nonprofessional musical production.

By the mid-1950's a few high schools, colleges, and community theatre groups were doing Broadway book musicals. The production rights to such shows seemed out of reach to most nonprofessional groups, and the costs involved sent many a dreaming musical producer back to the reality of his budgeted one-set play. (After all, *Our Town is* a great show.)

"So You're Doin' a Musical"

Then the revolution began! Around the author's neck of the woods (Ohio), it was the high schools that led the way. This was only natural. They had everything under one roof; the school orchestra, the dramatic club, and, quite often, a recently equipped stage to command the diversified sets required by most musical productions. Production budgets became a temporary investment in future profits rather than a monetary loss. More students could participate. Musical training broadened. And most amazing of all, there was greater audience reception, both among students and community citizens who previously had shunned amateur performances.

Colleges and universities were soon to overcome early interdepartmental difficulties and join music and drama upon the stages of numerous American campuses. Even the most successful collegiate groups found larger audiences for musical productions.

Early community theatre groups solved their biggest problem when they discovered that pianos or a piano and rhythm section could adequately replace an orchestra. Some

groups mustered up full orchestral accompaniment (often seeded with a few pro's who were glad to sit in for kicks or a few bucks under the table). And if all else failed, the local church organist could be counted on to supply the musical backing.

These *were* the early days of some of today's most proficient nonprofessional producers of musical comedies. These *are* the days for many groups just getting started in the field. These *could* be the days for many other groups who are planning their first musical production.

Finding Success Without a Map

Early amateurs found success; if not on stage, usually in the box office. As with any successful undertaking, the word spread. "Do a musical; you can't go wrong." Or, "If *they* can do a musical, why can't we?" Success was emulated but often missed, as group copied group. Play directors became directors of musical comedy. Variety show coordinators became directors of musical comedy. Band directors became directors of musical comedy. People who had seen the Broadway production became directors of musical comedy. But it is a good bet that a very small percentage of these directors of musical comedies actually had any specialized knowledge in directing a musical comedy. In their mind was a vision of what their production could be. In their heart there was a desire to bring Broadway to the community's door step. In their power was "play- or music-oriented" direction skills they had learned through formal education or from years of experience.

In reality these nonmusical-comedy directors realized different types of successful musical productions. The accent varied. Plays with music, choral programs with continuity, dance recitals with laughs, or showcases for superior orchestras—it all depended on where you were and what interest or talent was strongest in a particular group. But one fact was sure, each was a success under the guise of a Broadway-style musical.

Although some of these shows were real successes, most were definitely not. The real tragedy is when you consider that, with the proper planning and a little more organization, these productions could have been a rewarding experience in professionalism, both for players and audience.

Granted that most producers and directors recognize their shortcomings, how can production pitfalls be avoided? The answer is as simple as taking your audiences on a theatrical

Bye Bye Birdie, *J. S. Morton East High School, Cicero, Illinois, Jack L. Leckel, director.*

vacation. Pick an exciting destination and plot your course in a detailed itinerary of events.

PICKING THE RIGHT DESTINATION

To undertake a book musical is to assume a complex task that is unlike doing any play ever produced. Problems are to be expected and kept in mind, especially in the first musical production. Few organizations, if any, lick all the problems on their first try. Most groups learn from each show and rise to a high degree of professionalism. Of course, this is not to say that a first musical cannot be enjoyable or even professional. It *is* to say the planning and skills required for musicals are sufficiently different from plays that problems are a certainty. Even if this book were the complete answer, and producers followed it to the letter, the human factor would produce many errors on the first trial. Top Broadway professionals spend six to eight weeks, eight hours a day, plus a month of tryouts on the road to get a new musical ready for Broadway.

But, alas, there must always be a first. The most important fact is to learn from each show

and do a better job next time. Strive for technique, organization, and professionalism.

REASONS FOR DOING A MUSICAL

There are many reasons for doing a musical production. Here is a summary of the main ones:

- It offers specialized training in America's theatrical art form.
- As the big event of the year, it can help stir interest in other related activities.
- More people can take an active part (larger cast and production crew).
- Musicians are given the opportunity to play the best musical arrangements in popular music.
- Students and group members, unskilled at acting, can fulfill their theatrical expression as singers, dancers, or members of a precision production crew.
- There is a better chance of audience and financial success.
- Plus the reasons for doing a play.

Of course, there are also liabilities. If it wouldn't look so absurd on the jacket, this book might well be called "Overcoming the Liabilities and Living Up to the Responsibilities of Musical Theatre Production." It is a big job, but one that can be relatively easy when broken down into little *organized* parts. If the whole is not broken down into smaller parts it will remain too large an obstacle that could never reach its full potential. And although it is essential to break the whole down into organized workable parts, it is also necessary for the director to keep the *whole* in mind (preferably with *written* guidelines). In this way, when the parts are put back together into a finished production, the whole will have a uniform style and run smoothly as a unit.

When an audience comes to see any theatrical venture, it expects the production to transport it into the atmosphere intended by the playwright. Relatives come to a nonprofessional group's production just to see their Mary or Johnny perform, but even they can be won over to the side of entertainment.

Some self-deluded directors may feel their productions achieve the stature of a salable entertainment every time—and perhaps rightly so. It is possible, however, to work so close to a production that the problems seem to disappear. The best directors keep asking themselves how they can make the show better. They have a unique talent for being able to view each rehearsal with just as fresh an eye as will the audience the final product. They find mistakes in their work and change them. Too many directors act as if heeding the home permanent commercial, "Set it and forget it." Once a director realizes the complexities of musical production he is mentally ready to set his goal.

Some people say you can't expect professionalism from nonprofessionals. This author would be forced to agree. No one can expect professionalism from amateurs. No one can *get* professionalism from amateurs, unless they impose it on them first. Any capable director

ANDREW G. THOME

My Fair Lady, *Ursuline College, Louisville, Kentucky, Robert M. Fisher, director.*

can achieve professionalism with nonprofessional talent if he picks a reasonable show, allows enough time for concentrated training, and provides the proper direction and organization to back up the inexperienced actors, singers, and dancers.

Therefore, the target to aim for—the right destination—is professionalism. The next step is to chart the path carefully toward that goal. The time to chart that path is at least six months prior to the scheduled musical production. (Longer if the rehearsal schedule runs more than ten weeks.)

This lead time is necessary to provide the proper selection, planning, preproduction meetings, tryouts, casting, set construction, publicity, costumes, rehearsal, ticket sales, and the hundreds of other details covered in this book. Of all the groups that responded to the Musical Comedy Production Questionnaire, only six groups ever postponed a performance (then only because of severe weather or the assassination of the President) and none was ever canceled. This is a fine testimonial to the tradition of "the show must go on." Yet it is a sure bet that of the thousand or so musical productions these groups have presented, most could have used more time in preparation. The *evil of time* is the foe of professionalism. In too

many instances, the audience is left with just another show that, with more time, could have been much better. Should there have been more lead time? Not necessarily. Usually there is a lot of time in the early weeks of production during which people wait for things to jell. By putting this time to work, the fireworks of last-minute chaos will be defused, and the pressure of time running out will be greatly reduced. A better show will result because waste time is converted to productive time.

In a later chapter we will discuss each function of producing a musical, and how to capitalize on these early weeks, but before getting into that there are two prerequisites for a near-professional production. These are:

1) Selection of a musical that will be suitable for your group and audience.
2) Starting the production machinery before the show gets to the tryout stage.

The all-important background in selecting the most advantageous musical for your group to present will be covered in the following two chapters. An actual step-by-step musical comedy production system is detailed in Chapter III.

CHAPTER I Selection

*"I've Got a Great Idea,
  Let's Do . . ."*

The selection of the show and the days on which it is to be presented are two of the most important decisions any group producing a musical must make.

There are thousands of straight plays to choose from. Greek theatre, classic dramas of social injustice, Shakespearean greats, religious or historical plays, thrillers, light comedies—over twenty centuries of the spoken word from which to select. Play catalogs are chock-full of works from many nations. Consider further that the director has probably acted in countless plays and studied the field as part of his formal education. Yet picking a play to present is not an easy task. Serious directors go to great lengths to find just the *right* play.

Now consider the scope of the musical. It is much narrower. This art form is native to the United States. It can be directly traced back to the American minstrel shows of the 1850's. From this period, little more than the works of the last fifty years remain intelligible enough for present-day production.

The musical comedy form, as we know it today, wasn't completely born until *Oklahoma!* in 1943, which further narrows the field of selection to twenty-five years' work of one country (plus a handful of shows from abroad, mainly England).

To further complicate matters, musicals require large casts, a multitude of sets and costumes, a variety of talent, and a hefty production budget. Other problems such as stage limitations and community acceptance must also be considered.

The current selection offers only some 150 shows, which further complicates the *most important* decision a director will be called on to make: the title of the musical to be presented. The most difficult because he must try to consider all the factors in advance and envision, however vaguely, the means to a successful production.

To engage in any musical production, "feeling" that things will eventually work out is courting the type of folly that inevitably results in a haphazard presentation. Erroneous selection and insufficient rehearsal time are the chief causes of failure in nonprofessional musical comedy productions. And although not having enough time to make a show a hit is frustrating, picking the *wrong* show is hopeless!

How to Measure
What Will Be Successful

According to catalogs, every show is an outstanding Broadway success. Of course this is not true, but with few exceptions, each show could be a smash when presented under proper circumstances. A group that presents a musical only occasionally is wise to stick to the classic titles or the latest "hot" shows as they become available. However, a group that presents two or more musicals a year should consider some of the more obscure titles to provide fresh interest and variety.

There are many pros and cons to consider with regard to the type of musicals to be selected. Here are a few points that might be of interest.

Concerning the old chestnuts, you might hear such cries from members of your group as "That show has been done a thousand times!" Whereas most progressive groups prefer to do new shows, the old shows continue to be done because people enjoy seeing them. Shows such as *Oklahoma!* and *The King and I* will never die. As in the case of certain operas, people will pay to see them over and over.

Age and experience don't always go hand in hand. Neither do hits and the year they were written. The ageless quality of some older shows is helping them repeat their original success. *Show Boat, Oklahoma!, The Student Prince,* and scores of others are still pulling in large, appreciative audiences. Their writing and production styles are outdated, but the magnitude of their contribution to the world of musical entertainment will endear them to international audiences for many years to

W. HARLEY GROOM

EDHOLM & BLOMGREN PHOTOGRAPHERS

Many small musicals can be just as enjoyable as the larger shows. Examples are A Funny Thing Happened on the Way to the Forum, *staged by the Players Club, Columbus, Ohio, Gerald L. Ness, managing director;* Once Upon a Mattress, *directed by Ronald L. Reed at Lincoln Community Playhouse, Lincoln, Nebraska; and* The Fantasticks, *staged by the Dayton Players, Dayton, Ohio, Patrick S. Gilvary, director.*

come. They will find success in areas where they are new or areas in which they haven't been presented for a number of years. There is, however, a limit to the number of times a normal person will pay to see these or *South Pacific,* or even *My Fair Lady.*

Master moviemaker Walt Disney instituted a policy of re-releasing his top creative attractions on an average of about every seven years. His philosophy was that his audience changes on seven-year cycles and through the generations, avid fans will pay to see each of his productions five or more times. Likewise, perennial musicals will find new, younger audiences, as well as adults returning to view one of their favorites.

Another factor going for established works is their familiar music, which often becomes popular independent of the theatrical production. Music promotors and some psychologists have told us the average listener must hear a song at least three times before it really sinks in or becomes distinctive from other accepted music patterns. (This is also an important reason for the existence of overtures and underscoring of the musical's main themes throughout the score.)

Then there is the obvious reason for avoiding old standards that have been overdone. After a person has seen a show so many times, they won't come back to see it rehashed. Musicals that are largely unknown have the advantage of providing fresh and surprising material for audiences seeking entertainment not to be found elsewhere.

In progressive communities there is a distinct interest in what is new or more recent. It is difficult to assess entertainment value as to freshness or nostalgia. But given a choice, which would you rather see—*Oklahoma!* or *Hello, Dolly!? Oklahoma!* has more enduring songs, but a lot fewer people have seen *Hello, Dolly!*—and besides, it's very "in" to go see *Hello, Dolly!* As a general rule, put your money on what's new. Thinking in a four-year production cycle, three up-to-date shows to one older name show makes a fine ratio.

The fame of many musicals is often tied too closely to the show's opening-night reviews. Contradicting critical error are such shows as *West Side Story, The Sound of Music, Damn Yankees, The King and I, Bye Bye Birdie, Can-Can, Kismet, Flower Drum Song,* and other favorites that were saved from generally unfavorable or lukewarm reviews by large advance sales or strong word-of-mouth advertising. Conversely, there are many little-known shows such as *Goldilocks, A Family Affair,* and *Ernest in Love* that did not get good reviews and did not enjoy long runs amid sophisticated New York audiences, but would still be great shows for local audiences.

In short, Broadway shows don't always fail because they are poorly written. Bad directors, stars, and hasty producers have taken their toll of creative and entertaining musicals. Wise selection of one of these unheralded shows can be just as rewarding as doing a big-name show.

SOURCES OF INFORMATION
THAT INFLUENCE SELECTION

Where do directors turn when they want to do a musical? Here's how respondents to the Musical Comedy Production Questionnaire ranked the following influences:

Personal experience   112
Catalogs   71
Recommendation from someone else   64
Recordings   35
Others   3

All of these sources lend important background and, if possible, each one should be incorporated to narrow the field of possible scripts to be read and studied. The most useful and most dangerous of these sources is personal experience.

The other sources listed are usually carefully investigated, but there is a tendency to credit the personal mind with more knowledge than it actually possesses. Each prospective show must be carefully inspected and reviewed before final selection is made.

Scheduling a show the director "once enjoyed seeing," or favoring a certain title just because "all those great songs" came from it, without carefully examining its production feasibility, can easily end in a disastrous flop. When viewing an enjoyable musical production, it is very easy to overlook difficult aspects that would certainly stand out if unsuccessfully executed. Professionals earn their money making the difficult look easy. Mechanical stages or quick massive set changes may be essential to the pace of the production. Make sure you know what you are getting into *at the time* you are getting into it.

It also helps if directors *tune up* their personal experience by seeing as many musicals as possible. Movies, TV, summer stock, professional, or other nonprofessional productions are all good sources.

By using these means, the director can rapidly become more familiar with the entire field and easily find several shows that match the production capabilities at his disposal.

OBTAINING PERUSAL SCRIPTS
AND PERFORMANCE RIGHTS

It is best to reduce the complete array of suitable titles to two or three for final consideration. Scripts and conductors' scores may then be obtained from the agent leasing the individual titles. There are four main agents involved in leasing the rights to present musicals. These are as follows:

Tams-Witmark Music Library, Inc.
757 Third Avenue
New York, N.Y. 10017

Samuel French, Inc.
25 West 45th Street
New York, N.Y. 10036

Rodgers & Hammerstein Repertory
120 East 56th Street
New York, N.Y. 10022

Music Theatre International
119 West 57th Street
New York, N.Y. 10019

The charge for obtaining perusal scripts varies according to the policy of each company. Some require only the payment of postage. Others require a sizable deposit. In most cases scripts are not for sale. To avoid the expense and time delay involved in this process, it is wise to check for a possible published text. Over the years a number have been published in magazines and hard-bound volumes that might be available in your local library.

Perusal copies are requested from the leasing agent by means of special forms supplied with their catalogs or by sending the following information with your request: the number of performances, production dates, admission prices, and seating capacity.

ing out, leaving distracting "holes" in the audience.

3) If the royalty quoted by the leasing agent is in excess of the production budget, notify the agent of this fact before dropping the show. If that particular show is

Send for Reading Copies of musicals

Please send me perusal books and scores and royalty and rental information on the following shows. I understand that I can keep the books and scores for two weeks—and that I will be obligated in no way except to pay the postal charges both ways.

I have checked or written in the titles of the shows I want to read.

- [ ] BYE BYE BIRDIE
- [ ] CAMELOT
- [ ] FINIAN'S RAINBOW
- [ ] BRIGADOON
- [ ] LI'L ABNER
- [ ] 110 IN THE SHADE
- [ ] MY FAIR LADY
- [ ] BELLS ARE RINGING
- [ ] OLIVER!
- [ ] CARNIVAL
- [ ] KISS ME KATE
- [ ] FUNNY GIRL

Other shows I want to read (Fill in titles).

D8 [ ] Send complete full color catalog

Please Print or Type

Your Name .... Title ....
Name of Your School or Organization ....
Street and Number ....
City and State .... Zip Code ....
Your Telephone Number Before 5 P.M. ....
After 5 P.M. ....
Capacity of Auditorium ....
Dates and Number of Performances ....
Expected Attendance at Each Performance ....
Admission Prices .... Is an Orchestration Required? ....

(Figure 1-1)   Musical Application Form

Royalties differ according to the title and group, and a certain amount of negotiations is required. The cost is based primarily on the number of people that will see your show and is not the familiar set price used for paying royalties on straight plays.

In dealing with these agents, you must represent a business interest—your budget. Some important points to remember are:

1) There is a definite market of supply and demand. If the show is in demand, the price (royalty) is higher. Usually these are the most recent shows, and if one group won't do them, some other group will. Therefore, by picking an older show that is new to your area and not in demand, you will find the agent will tend to charge a lower royalty to get the material in use rather than leave it sitting on the shelf.

2) If the performance is to be held in an auditorium with a capacity beyond your needs, a portion should be closed off and only the seating capacity to be used should be submitted to the leasing agent. This also prevents patrons from spread-

not in demand, the agent might consider a special arrangement at a reduced royalty.

FINAL SELECTION

The chief points to consider in picking a successful musical are as follows:

1) Ability to cast the show
2) Ability to assemble a capable production staff
3) Ability to mount a suitable production
4) Local audience acceptance
5) Costs

ABILITY TO CAST THE SHOW

A director can never be sure how a show will turn out until it opens its run. It is not unusual to have a shaky production right through dress rehearsal and still have a presentable show on opening night. Yet the director must foresee a means of filling the number of parts called for in his selection—even if that selection is six months to a year from actual production. It is amazing how talented people pop up in the strangest places, but each musical has certain fundamental personnel requirements. *Annie Get Your Gun* is a sure-fire hit if you have a good Annie and a sure flop if you haven't. A director seeking a successful production of *Annie Get Your Gun* should have at least one strong female lead

SWAYZE STUDIO

lined up to play the part of Annie before he schedules the title.

Also, he must foresee a means to musical accompaniment. Some groups are afforded the luxury of trying out musicians for their choice orchestra chairs—whereas others must search neighboring communities to fill their needs. A musical must have music. It is the primary resource to be found prior to further planning of any title.

ABILITY TO ASSEMBLE A CAPABLE PRODUCTION STAFF

To stage a musical properly, it is best to have an individual to fill each position mentioned in Chapter III. Although a given person may have the talent to perform many of these functions, the production will have a much better chance of success if he performs only the one in which he is most specifically skilled. Performing multiple functions may be a higher form of self-accomplishment, but it deprives the specialized supervision essential with nonprofessionals. Skills in other production functions should be used to their full potential in preproduction meetings, such as the counseling and guidance to the person who will actually perform the function.

Minimum requirements for a musical production staff are as follows:

1) An experienced stage director—a musical is no place to learn basic staging techniques.
2) A musical director capable of orchestral and choral direction.
3) A choreographer capable of transferring music into suitable dance patterns.
4) A competent technical director to train inexperienced production staff members and supervise their activities.

Of course it is more advantageous to have a larger and more experienced staff, but with careful planning and team effort a successful musical show can be presented with this minimal backbone of experienced help.

ABILITY TO MOUNT A SUITABLE PRODUCTION

A suitable production may be presented in any style or form (i.e. realistic, impressionistic, in-the-round, proscenium, etc.) as long as they are completely carried through. Too often, for example, impressionism is used as an excuse for something incomplete. Except for shows such as *The Fantasticks* or *Stop the World–I Want to Get Off,* in which the writing is highly stylized, realistic rather than suggested settings are usually more effective; and they don't pose as big a problem as one might think.

It is not logical to spend thousands of man hours in cast and orchestra rehearsals and then present the fruits of the toil in front of the regular auditorium drapes. *Any group accepting the challenge of presenting a musical inherits the responsibility of giving their audience what they have paid to see: a well-paced musical show with tasteful sets, colorful costumes, and adequate lighting.* If a group cannot mount such a production, they should consider a one-set drama or a variety show, which could include hit songs and sketches from many musicals. For without proper mood-creating and -holding devices, most musicals will drag.

LOCAL AUDIENCE ACCEPTANCE

There are two schools of thought in theatrical production today. The first is that a group must educate their audience as well as the players. Second, that the group and the show they present provide an entertaining diversion—a vacation from reality to another place-in-being where the audience finds fun, excitement, and, perhaps, a few sentimental tears. Often, there is no clear-cut line between these two schools, but individuals tending to one side are usually quick to state their objections to the other. People who embrace both are difficult to find. Remove all the emotional arguments about how each school is wrecking theatre and only one conclusion can be drawn: People have different tastes in entertainment.

Entertainment tastes are not the same in any one community, let alone all the communities of the nation. A variety of tastes is exhibited on Broadway because New York (and a few other large cities) is big enough to tolerate them all. *Milk and Honey,* for example, is written for Jewish appeal, and with largely "inside" Jewish audiences, it ran for

Larger shows allow many more people to get into the act, and their variety may range from the strong vocal musical Oklahoma!, *staged by the Hill Country Arts Foundation, Ingram, Texas, directed by William Y. Hardy, to the powerful dancers' show* West Side Story, *directed by Robert J. Phillips at Thornton Fractional South High School, Lansing, Illinois.*

Paint Your Wagon, directed by Maris U. Ubans at California State College at Los Angeles, Los Angeles, California; and Little Me, directed by Jack L. Leckel for J. S. Morton East High School, Cicero, Illinois. Not so well known as some other musicals, these can still make great productions if well tailored to your group. Such shows can also lend freshness to a group that presents musicals on a regular basis.

more than a year. Nonprofessional groups presenting *Milk and Honey* without a predominantly Jewish audience would be sure to experience failure simply because their patrons would not completely understand what they were seeing. On the other hand, *Fiddler on the Roof* has the same (and probably an even stronger) Jewish appeal, but is so universal in its presentation that anyone, even without the slightest understanding of Jewish ways, can enjoy and learn from this musical masterpiece.

Likewise, such ingredients as sophistication, sex, language, suggestive moves, location, and music must be taken into account when selecting a show for local consumption. Some theatrical people scoff at the idea of "lowering" themselves to the audience's level, but it's a rare director who can build local audiences by giving them what they don't want to see. Adverse publicity may sell the latest "hot" paperback in abundance, but it can turn the churchgoing people away in droves.

Not too long ago a young midwestern lass, playing Lola in *Damn Yankees,* was the target of national publicity when her local minister took to his pulpit to chastise the girl for her suggestive dancing. *Damn Yankees* is one of the best musicals available. Its sequence of scenes alternating full stage settings with drops (drop-set-drop-set-drop, etc.), lends itself to production in the average high-school auditorium. However, Lola is a devil, an accomplished seductress, and 172 years old. Although she appears much younger in the show, there is a real question as to the acceptability of a high-school teenager sufficiently experienced to give the part its just due. Disregarding the minister's attack for moral reasons, it is safe to say that 16-year-old girls will always be far more successful entertainers in *Bye Bye Birdie, My Fair Lady, Li'l Abner,* or *Carousel* than they would be in *Damn Yankees, Irma La Douce,* or *Sweet Charity.*

Audiences, particularly local audiences, can be embarrassed. Give them a good show with embarrassing moments and the word of mouth will be of the embarrassment, not of how good the show was. Risqué shows have a place in universities and little-theatre production, but not in high school. However, what is risqué may be a matter of local interpretation or might be successfully handled by directorial restraint or cutting. Productions of *Guys and Dolls, Fanny, The Fantasticks,* offer material that could be difficult in high-school production, yet the fun of *Guys and Dolls* and the beauty in the others can be presented successfully without seeming low or offensive.

Costs

Broadway is the center of creativity and the birthplace of the musical comedy repertory. New ideas and shows are presented in the liberal atmosphere that has made it the theatrical capital of the world. Theoretically, there is only one prerequisite for getting a promising work before the public: the money necessary to get it produced. When money is available there is a surplus of competent actors, singers, dancers, and production people to put it to work. On the nonprofessional level, financial backing is not nearly as important to success, yet must be considered carefully.

All musicals are fully protected and subject to royalties. These royalty costs run approximately six times the cost of a play of comparable popularity. There is an additional material rental charge of approximately $100. This covers the use of musical orchestrations, chorus books, director materials, and sides (incomplete scripts with only lines and five-word cues for each part).

Physical production costs are about five to eight times higher than for a play. Multiple sets, costuming a larger cast (often with several changes), extra lighting, bigger promotion, and the hundreds of other costly little details add up to a sizable total expenditure, usually ranging from $2,000 to $6,000, depending on the organization and the length of the run.

Commenting on higher costs, one Indiana director said, "Musicals are expensive and time-consuming. It costs us five to six times the cost of a straight play, but they (musicals) are the most popular show of any season."

In the national Musical Comedy Production Questionnaire survey of 155 groups, 95 percent reported all their musical productions met expenses or made a financial profit.

Although profit should never be the absolute goal of any nonprofessional group (particularly a school group), it is healthy for the growth of the organization and an indisputable measure of success. It is the means to better productions and larger audiences. Even the proponents of education for art's sake cannot deny this success, as unartistic as it may sometimes appear to them.

Comparing financial success and the educational advantages of theatrical achievement is like comparing apples and oranges. They're just not the same thing. And, of course, doing a musical never guarantees financial success.

Musicals can help the cost situation in other ways. A well-rounded theatrical program for any group is about three or four productions a year. Two or three plays and one musical.

For some musicals, it is important to have actors that physically fit the part, as in this production of L'il Abner, *by the summer workshop of Beaverton High School, Beaverton, Oregon, directed by Robert R. Buseick.*

The musical, with proven superior audience draw, can then be used to sell season tickets and improve crowds for straight plays. Regardless of whether a subscription series is offered, profits or reserved budget monies derived from the musical can be used to provide play productions on a grander scale.

The process of presenting a musical is like that of running a business. It must be considered as such if the producing group is to grow and prosper. The producing group must cope with the procedures of setting up a company, selecting management, hiring workers, building and operating a plant. So it has been in the theatrical past, so it is with each new Broadway production, and so it will continue to be for all groups in the future.

The money for each production must come from somewhere, it must be handled, and the results (profit or loss) must be accounted for.

(Figure 1-2)

COSTS TO OPENING NIGHT FOR A RECENT BROADWAY MUSICAL

SCENERY

Designing	$7,000	
Painting and Building	72,600	
Miscellaneous Purchases and Expenses	1,700	
TOTAL		$81,300
Props Purchases and Rentals		21,800
Costumes		103,000
Electrical and Sound Equipment		15,500

DIRECTOR

Stage and Assistant	$4,200	
Choreography and Assistant	4,200	
Vocal Coaching and Arranging	8,000	
TOTAL		$16,400

REHEARSAL EXPENSES

Salaries:

Principals	$7,200	
Singers	7,200	
Dancers	10,400	
Company Crew	10,000	
Stagehands	16,700	
Wardrobe and Dressers	2,800	
Pianist	3,400	
Musicians and Conductor	12,000	
Production Secretary	400	
Stage Managers	5,000	
	$75,100	
Theatre Expenses and Rent	4,500	
Scripts and Parts	800	
Miscellaneous	1,000	
TOTAL		$81,400

PRELIMINARY ADVERTISING

Press Agent Salary and Expenses	$2,900	
Newspaper Advertising	11,700	
Outdoor Advertising	1,300	
Photos and Signs	5,200	
Mailing	2,000	
Printing	5,000	
TOTAL		$28,100
Company and General Manager		3,800
Office Expenses		2,800
Producers Fee		2,400
Legal Fees and Disbursements		12,200
Auditing Fees		750
Railroad and Transportation		6,500
Hotel and Living Expenses		8,400
Payroll Taxes		3,400
Carting		3,500
Music Orchestrations, etc.		40,000
Contract Cancellation		350
Insurance		1,000
Welfare and Pension Funds		3,900
Miscellaneous and Telephone		3,900
TOTAL PRODUCTION COSTS		$440,400

Cost for a nonprofessional revival may be less than 1/500th that of bringing in the original Broadway version. The expense of professional productions and the costly unions with which they must deal won't be encountered by most amateur groups. Business overhead is also much lower. Broadway must endure the expenses of trial and error involved in doing a show for the first time: costly charges for rewriting, duplicating music, and reworking sets.

Even so, a knowledge of how a Broadway producer spends his money provides proportionate guidelines for setting up a local production budget.

It is interesting to note that the third largest single expense is $40,000 for the orchestration and music-copying charges—one of the many expenses found only in first-time Broadway productions and of no concern to the nonprofessional revival producer.

In fact, if it had been possible to have a non-pro group present this show on Broadway, it would have cut the costs in half. This figure is based on all members' contributing their services, but still allows the purchase of all the production materials from professional suppliers. Eliminating the labor and creative expense from these materials, the total cost would then be reduced to about $8,000 or $10,000.

Of course, that's like saying the human body is worth only 62¢, but if the talent exists in your group, it is entirely possible to copy the original Broadway production for a lot less. This underscores the major expense in any undertaking of this nature: people's time and talent. If talented people are willing to contribute time, just about anything can be accomplished. In most cases this much time will not be available. Nor will most groups want to cope with the tremendous complexities of the original production. If they do, however, actual Broadway sets, drops, and costumes can be rented for a fraction of the costs listed in the example.

The costs of a professional-looking production are not that expensive. Certainly not worth the expensive loss of prestige endured in a shabbily mounted one.

If a group follows these five points of final selection, there will be no need to ask the question, "Will this show sell tickets?" The question is automatically answered when you have chosen the best possible show your group can do. Promotion will still be necessary, but by choosing the show that fits your group you have the best ticket-seller for a nonprofessional production—a good show.

SETTING THE PRODUCTION DATES

It would be nice to be able to see into the future to find out which performance dates would be best: Heavy rain, a bad snow, or even a real nice balmy evening keeps would-be theatregoers in the comfort of their own homes. Such factors happen or they don't. No one has control over them.

On the other hand, a number of other factors may be anticipated, and it is well to do so. The fewer things that will be taking place on your performance dates, the more people will be free to attend. If possible, avoid conflicts with such events as large community or school activities, county fairs, elections, large sports activities, holiday weekends, and other theatrical events. Helpful in the task of long-range date-picking are Chamber of Commerce social calendars, fine arts council programs, city or county booking registers for civic auditoriums, and the like. If the production is planned for two weekends, make sure the first has fewer conflicts.

Of course, the dates of production should allow enough time for proper scheduling, casting, and rehearsal.

ENGLISH SHOWS

The musicals *Oliver, Stop the World—I Want to Get Off, Half-a-Sixpence,* and others originally premiered in London and were imported to the United States. Because of their success in this country they are available through New York leasing agents. Similarly, production rights for many American musicals are available in England from agencies comparable to the ones in America (usually only the ones that have subsequently played London).

Many fine English productions, however, were not imported. Such shows as *Blitz,* an outstanding musical by Lionel Bart, which tells a moving story of England during World War II bombing, are considered financial risks because of "limited" story appeal. Since many Broadway musicals the size of *Blitz* must run for nine months to a year at capacity to break even, this is probably justified. But *Blitz* would be a great "new" musical for numerous U.S. groups.

Then there are such shows as *Pickwick* and *Lock Up Your Daughters,* which enjoyed several years of success in London but didn't make the grade in this country. Like *Blitz,* these shows are not available in this country, and at the time of writing there is no easy way to import performance rights or production materials. English groups wishing to do cer-

A number of musicals from TV, movies, and other non-Broadway sources are being tailored for nonprofessional production. Some talented groups are even writing their own. Examples are Cinderella, directed by Ray S. Canaday at Grand Junction High School, Grand Junction, Colorado; and The Song of Solomon Grundy, staged by the Chanticleer Players, Council Bluffs, Iowa, and directed by Norman Filbert.

tain American titles are faced with the same problem.

The only solution is for local nonprofessional producers to watch the London scene (through *Variety, Play & Players Magazine* [English], or other trade journals) for musicals that they think would make good local productions. Then make several requests for information about these titles to New York leasing agents. If enough requests are received, they will see the show as a profitable venture and conclude the necessary arrangements to make the show available in this country.

It is highly possible that some of the world's finest musical shows may someday make their American debut on a college campus or in a major community theatre.

FOLLOWING THROUGH ON SUCCESSFUL SELECTION

Acclaimed success is only one reason for picking the right musical. Managing to fill all the available seats, getting ten curtain calls, and having everybody's friends and relatives preach on the "Broadway show they saw at . . ." does not, in itself, constitute a success. Success is never to be measured by what a group *takes* from an audience, but rather what it *gives* them. In fact, it is quite easy to find successful flops. Whenever a show falls short of what it could have been, it is a flop. This is the only way a show's production, either play or musical, can be judged. Plays usually come off according to the level of talent inherent in the cast and production staff, but musicals often fall short of the mark. *Time is the villain*. The vast number of tasks involved in musicals, in too many cases, prevent the show from rising to its full potential. As you move into the production chapters, you will see why the lack of proper rehearsal time and proper planning has scuttled more musical productions than all the bad singers, dancers, actors, and musicians put together.

Learn a more effective use of time, and a better musical show will be the result.

In achieving these heights, the cast and production team give their audience a top product. Simultaneously they are scoring the biggest success of all: building the favorable reputation that will bring their audiences back for the sake of pure entertainment, not just to see friends or relatives. In the process, new audiences are created by favorable word of mouth. Maybe not after one show, but in the long run surely. When a group is known for its professional-like productions, be it little theatre, university, or high school, even the hard-nosed professional theatregoers will find it difficult to stay away.

Each selection is important—to the success of the production and to the long-term success of a group's reputation for doing good theatre.

The sure way to provide the success of each selection is to know what is available; survey the available talent and production facilities; select a musical within the capabilities of the group; make sure that selection fits the environment in which it is to be presented; and ensure enough time to allow the group to achieve its full potential before opening night closes in.

CHAPTER II History

"ABCD—EFG—HIJK—LMNOP
QRS and TUV—W and XYZ;
Now You've Heard My ABC'S
Tell Me What You Think of Me"

Many students find history books "deadly dull," yet thrive on the movies or TV documentaries on the very subjects they are studying. For those who prefer visual history, rest assured that this chapter is not a history of musical comedy.

Not that studying one of the histories of musical comedy isn't good background for a successful musical production. It is strongly encouraged, especially for those who are involved in selection. There are four main works in this area: *Musical Comedy in America* by Cecil Smith, a most authoritative volume covering a year-by-year history from the birth of early concepts of musical comedy to 1950; *The World of Musical Comedy* by Stanley Green, kept fairly up-to-date by a man who has counted the great names of modern musical comedy as personal friends; *Complete Book of the American Musical Theater* by David Ewen, a general show-by-show history of the more important musicals complete through its publication in 1958; and *The American Musical Theater* by Lehman Engel.

In reality, this chapter deals with the interpretation of musical theatre history, why it is important to know when the show was originally presented, and why the various changes over the years must be understood in order to present a successful revival production. Understanding these factors compensates for the time lag between the original and revival production. (A guide to where to modernize, if you like!) The newer the show, the less of this "time interpretation" will be required.

MUSIC IN THE THEATRE

Did you ever ask yourself, "Why does musical theatre exist?" Probably not, yet the answer is basic to the complete understanding of musical characters and the musical comedy form of theatre—and the reason for the crazy subtitle for this chapter.

The various musical "feelings" are emotions that can't be put into mere words. Musical composition records a naturalness in man that can't be preserved in any other way. It is not dependent on every individual's personal interpretation of the word "happiness" or what is the meaning of sadness. When music is performed correctly it automatically conveys the emotion intended by the composer. In the same sense music is the greatest actor of all time because it is always right in its part. When music is combined with a dramatic movement it is a tremendous help to an actor developing his part. When he becomes "musically correct" and achieves the musical naturalness *written* into the score, he will usually find that he has nearly accomplished dramatic perfection within the musical number.

Musical naturalness works in other ways, too. Throughout the score it helps build emotion. For example, did you ever watch an old movie Western without background music? It doesn't seem natural. Yet, when you watch a modern movie you don't even notice that the thunderous chase is about three-fourths music.

Today just about *everything* has a musical background—especially the TV commercial.

This musical naturalness also can be found in religions, in the rhythms of primitive tribes, in teaching the ABC's and nursery rhymes, in a military battle charge, and as a soothing background in offices and factories, plus thousands of other instances when a certain point or emotion needs to be emphasized. (Some farmers even claim they can increase egg production by playing music to their chickens.) In fact, the very existence of music had to come from a want or a need to express this type of emotion. It was destined that one day music and theatre should get together.

From a technical viewpoint, the Greek chorus was probably the first form of musical theatre. However, the first *musical* theatre to

PHIL FLAD JR.

Shows of the 1940's and early 1950's tend to have fewer sets because of the writing and production practices of the time. Examples are The Boy Friend *(3 sets), directed by Maris U. Ubans at California State College at Los Angeles, Los Angeles, California;* Finian's Rainbow *(2 sets), directed by Richard L. Sutch at Mamaroneck High School, Mamaroneck, New York; and* Wonderful Town *(5–6 sets), produced by University of Dayton Players, Dayton, Ohio, and directed by Patrick S. Gilvary.*

establish itself firmly was Italy's grand opera. Although there have been many different moods within this form, the form has remained basically the same for hundreds of years.

As a result of the search for a musical theatre form lighter than grand opera, the Viennese operetta was born. Next came the *comic operas* of Gilbert and Sullivan. Many people argue that both departures were merely steps in the development of musical comedy. Perhaps so, but to this author they will always be regarded in a class by themselves. Certainly new comic operas are still being written. And although operettas were more a product of

the society of the times, the form was unique and employed mainly one style of music. Both, however, are considered connecting links between grand opera and musical comedy.

THE EVOLUTION OF THE AMERICAN MUSICAL COMEDY

America's first attempt at theatrical expression through music was the minstrel show— a far cry from modern musical comedy, but stemming straight from the musical naturalness of our young country.

The decades that followed found musical theatre going through various moods, styles,

The Sound of Music, *directed by Theora Bartholomew at Bakersfield High School, Bakersfield, California; and* Camelot, *directed by Jack Nakano at Santa Barbara High School, Santa Barbara, California. Massive set changes were made possible in such shows as these with the introduction of mechanical stages. A good duplication or substitute for this technology is essential to a successful presentation of such productions.*

TIM PUTZ PHOTOGRAPHY

Bakersfield High School production of The Sound of Music.

Santa Barbara, California High School production of Camelot using the original Broadway scenery.

and trends. Pantomime, burlesque, revue, and vaudeville quickly replaced the "extravaganza" that is given general credit as the first formal step in the development of what we now call musical comedy.

The most important branch in the family tree was the revue. George M. Cohan took this basic form and worked it into loosely constructed story lines.

After that came Irving Berlin, Jerome Kern, and Richard Rodgers and Moss Hart. Soon to be followed by Cole Porter, the teams of Rodgers and Oscar Hammerstein II; Alan Jay Lerner and Frederick Loewe; and Dick Adler and Jerry Ross; plus Frank Loesser, Leonard Bernstein, Jule Styne, Meredith Willson, and a host of others.

Related to time, there are two main periods: 1914 to 1943: the final experimentation in the development of a unique theatrical musical form—a formula that could frame many musical styles and still remain modern as time passed by; and 1943 to the present: how this established form has been put to use.

This book deals almost exclusively with the period since 1943. If your group is planning to do a show from the earlier period, it (with rare exception) will need a complete overhaul in regard to pruning dialogue, updating jokes, revising production suggestions that appear in the script, and so on.

MODERN MUSICAL COMEDY

When *Oklahoma!* opened at the St. James Theatre on March 31, 1943, it signaled the decline and/or fall of all other musical theatre formulas. Its coming was gradual. Such shows as *Showboat, On Your Toes,* and *Pal Joey* foretold its arrival, but that opening night unveiled the basic formula that is still being reworked today.

Oklahoma! has since become dated. The songs are still current (and will probably live forever); the book isn't as deep as those of the musicals that are selling today, but the real difference is the way these two elements are merged together. The fact that this material was assembled for production in 1942–43 is the big drawback. The same goes for just about every other musical available for nonprofessional production. The following paragraphs touch on some of the trends of musical comedy since *Oklahoma!* established the basic form.

Musical "feeling" and/or the naturalness of music doesn't change, but the means of expressing them do. For example, a baby shows discontent by crying; a child by pouting or throwing a temper tantrum; a juvenile by not cooperating; a mature adult by finding the best possible solution. Similar "growing pains" are reflected in the development of musical creativity and production.

Besides conveying musical moods differently, authors and composers keep finding new things to sing and dance about. The saying, "They're not writing songs like that anymore" is somewhat true in modern musical theatre. The loose construction of revues and early musical comedies enabled authors to drop in a good song about anything—anywhere in the show. It's no longer possible to have a "hit-parade" evening. (A big reason is that a true "hit parade" no longer exists.)

The result has been real theatrical music with, in most cases, greater meaning. Such great scores as *West Side Story, Gypsy, The Music Man, My Fair Lady, Fiddler on the Roof, The Fantasticks, Man of La Mancha,* and many other works were written for dramatic content, not the jukebox.

Such musicals as *Hello, Dolly!, Can-Can, Li'l Abner, The Boy Friend, Bye Bye Birdie, Stop the World–I Want to Get Off,* and others are still written *around* musical numbers. They were successful on individual qualities, similar to earlier shows. If they are to succeed in modern revival productions, those qualities had better be there.

For the most part, however, newer shows are written that are much tighter in construction. One, if not the biggest, production problem a local group faces is that of making tight construction work. The chapters on direction and settings cover construction problems in detail, but while on the general subject it would be well to mention that the writing construction of a musical is somewhat different from the construction of a play or novel. In the latter two cases, construction refers to the interweaving of the plot, subplots, character development, and exposition. Musical theatre construction is generally taken to mean the relationship and workability between plot, subplot, etc., and musical song and dance. This is a twist in the commonly held definition of construction that prevents a musical from becoming an opera at one extreme or a straight play at the other.

Other intangible factors include a trend toward more sophisticated writing and development of a more serious subject. Here again are elements that discourage half-hearted production.

On the tangible side there are all the improvements in production techniques that have taken place since Curly and Laurey first bounced across the stage in their "Surrey With the Fringe on Top." As you learn to use the *production guide* described in Chapter III, you will see how this affects whole scenes, and how you can improve your production by inserting new techniques found throughout the production function chapters.

CHAPTER III The Production Staff

"Not Wanted: A Shakespeare
With Baton and Taps"

Throughout theatrical history there have been rare individuals who have written, produced, and directed their own achievements. Among these were Aristophanes, William Shakespeare, Eugene O'Neill, Peter Ustinov, and Orson Welles.

When it comes to musicals, Victor Herbert, George M. Cohan, George Abbott, and Frank Loesser have all performed more than the usual number of creative, managerial, and production functions. But this author has yet to discover a single superhuman professional who has ever attempted to be producer, director, choreographer, musical director, conductor, and stage manager rolled into one.

MUSICALS REQUIRE A COMPLETE STAFF

When a group puts on a play there is a producer, director, and small production crew. The producer and director could logically be the same individual. His sphere of responsibility could also encompass supervision of a small production crew. But when a group produces a musical, there can be only one means of production management—a complete production staff. Even if one individual is the best expert in every step of production, he could never give his best to all the functions required to present a successful musical. Not even the most skillful professional has ever attempted such a foolhardy feat.

The production staff is best described *as a group of individuals providing independent creative efforts within a predetermined production plan under the guidance of the director, who has final say on all aspects of the production.* It must work in harmony with systematic precision toward the common goal—a successful musical production.

The members of the complete nonprofessional musical production staff are as follows:

Producer-Director
Choreographer
Musical Director

Stage Manager
Technical Director
Stage Crew Manager
Set Designer and Set Construction Supervisor
Wardrobe Mistress
Lighting and Special Effects Technician
Properties Master
Business Manager
Publicity and Promotion Director
Box Office Manager

Special sections will be devoted to each of these functions as they pertain to musicals, but first it is important to discuss how the group works as a unit before detailing their individual duties and responsibilities.

Of course, the first step is to have the musical selected before any meetings of the production staff are called. The time of the first meeting depends on the production schedule, but the group should usually meet at least a month to six weeks before the first scheduled rehearsal. The object of these meetings is to become familiar with the show, decide on set designs, iron out artistic differences, establish characterizations, outline production guidelines, and set a conservative, but firm, production schedule.

BECOMING FAMILIAR WITH THE SHOW

"The play's the thing" and the *whole* thing. None of its parts constitutes the whole. No special emphasis should be unduly placed on any one scene or musical number. Plan enough time to get the *whole* job done. As the chief creative source and presiding officer in charge of the production staff, the director should take the initial steps to bring the *whole* into focus for the entire group. The tool for accomplishing this task is a musical comedy *production guide.*

The musical comedy production guide is a written or typed schedule of the most important elements in any given musical. Its chief purpose is to provide a method of preplanning whereby paper is made to do the work of people. By doing so, costly mistakes are avoided and countless hours are saved.

The musical comedy production guide is prepared in four steps. The first step is simple, to read the script through two or three times. The next step is to construct the *rundown sheet*. This sheet is nothing more than a synopsis of scenes that also lists the musical numbers in their proper sequence. It might already exist. If so, you can find the rundown sheet information listed in the script introductory material. If the synopses of scenes and musical numbers are listed separately, it is a simple matter to combine the two.

With this basic information firmly in mind (and hand) proceed to the third step—researching the musical you are going to present.

MUSICAL COMEDY RUNDOWN SHEET
THE MUSIC MAN
(Figure 3-1)
ACT I.

PROLOGUE
SCENE 1. A Railway Coach. Morning, July 4, 1912.
  "Rock Island"
SCENE 2. River City, Iowa. Center of Town. Immediately following.
  "Iowa Stubborn"
  "Trouble"
SCENE 3. The Paroos' House. That evening.
  "Piano Lesson"
  "Goodnight My Someone"
SCENE 4. Madison Gymnasium. Thirty minutes later.
  "Seventy-Six Trombones"
  "Sincere"
SCENE 5. Exterior of Madison Library. Immediately following.
  "The Sadder-But-Wiser Girl"
  "Pickalittle"
  "Goodnight Ladies"
SCENE 6. Interior of Madison Library. Immediately following.
  "Marian the Librarian"
SCENE 7. A Street. The following Saturday noon.
SCENE 8. The Paroos' Porch. That evening.
  "My White Knight"
SCENE 9. Center of Town. Noon, the following Saturday.
  "Wells Fargo Wagon"

ACT II.
SCENE 1. Madison Gymnasium. The following Tuesday evening.
  "It's You"
  "Shipoopi"
  "Pickalittle" reprise.
SCENE 2. The Hotel Porch. The following Wednesday evening.
  "Lida Rose"
  "Will I Ever Tell You"
SCENE 3. The Paroos' Porch. Immediately following.
  "Gary, Indiana"
SCENE 4. The Footbridge. Fifteen minutes later.
  "It's You" reprise.
  "Till There Was You"
SCENE 5. A Street. Immediately following.
  "Seventy-Six Trombones"
  "Goodnight My Someone"
SCENE 6. Madison Park. A few minutes later.
  "Till There Was You" reprise.
SCENE 7. River City High School Assembly Room. Immediately following.
  "Finale"

Two hours in most public libraries can produce the following: The original review from the New York *Times;* magazine reviews from *Time, Life, Newsweek,* and other national magazines with regular theatre sections; photographs from Daniel Blum's yearly and composite *Theatre World* yearbooks; feature articles and photo stories from theatre publications such as *Theatre Arts, Show, Show Business Illustrated,* and *Theatre.* Many musical scripts are also published in illustrated hardbound editions. The *Reader's Guide* for the period in which the show opened will yield a wealth of information.

The ideal means to this end would be to get hold of souvenir programs, but this is often difficult, particularly where older shows are concerned. Record jackets are also good sources if they contain pictures of the professional version.

This step is important in that it provides additional information and visual understanding as to sets, costumes, and makeup. Such research can also provide important clues to choreography and direction. Its fruits can help prevent misconceptions of what the authors intended and obvious production blunders. It is

Scenes from Peter Pan, *presented by Beaverton High School, Beaverton, Oregon, and directed by Robert R. Buseick. Adjudged one of the country's outstanding productions and performed at a convention of the National Thespian Society, the show owed its success to a talented and hard-working production staff. Everyone knew what was to be done, and each did his share to perfection.*

wise to remember that the authors had a strong hand in the original production. It's a good bet that they tried other approaches before they decided on the final product. Prime your own creative effort by careful research from all available sources.

STRIKING THE COMMON DENOMINATOR

One of the most important factors in developing a musical production is to preserve the individual creativity of each member of the production staff. However, everybody is not doing his own show. Basic guidelines must be decided in advance.

How many people are to be on stage? Will there be enough room for the dancers? Should the settings be realistic or impressionistic? Will the show be played for laughs? Will there be any deletions in the script? Will any music need to be transposed? What should happen in this dance number? How does each production staff member visualize the scene? How should the costumes look? How will each character be portrayed? All these questions lend themselves to artistic differences. If conflicts are to be avoided during rehearsals, some means of resolving these differences is needed.

Therefore, the final step is to prepare the actual *Production Guide*. The production guide is a complete production "blueprint" prepared by the director prior to the pre-production meetings of the production staff. When it is completed, the director has a comprehensive picture of the *whole*. It also provides a means by which the other members of his staff can see the *whole* show as he does. It also provides a physical tool with which they can add, subtract, or otherwise adjust as they see fit. When a director furnishes each production staff member a copy of the production guide for study, artistic differences and/or suggestions are bound to come out. Then these differences can be worked out *before* rehearsals start and the production can proceed full speed ahead with unity, purpose, and understanding—attributes that are often missing when each member of the production staff is left to interpret the script by himself.

PREPARING THE PRODUCTION GUIDE

The production guide is built from the musical comedy rundown sheet. Information from the rundown sheet becomes the left-hand column of the production guide and subject matter on which all further entries are based.

To prepare the production guide by hand you will need one or two large sheets of paper or posterboard about 22″ x 28″. Sheets from a drawing tablet, chart paper, or wrapping paper would all do nicely. If you are composing the production guide on standard 8½″ x 11″ paper by means of a typewriter, set your tabulator for seven columns, each 16 spaces wide, with two spaces between each column. Other forms in which the production guide can be prepared are as follows: 1) on legal size paper to allow more typing space per column; 2) on duplicated forms; 3) on individual sheets for each scene, or 4) any combination of these methods that best suits the particular show and materials available. But presenting the material on one large sheet for each act is probably the best method because it portrays the *whole* better than any of the others.

Regardless of the presentation form, list the rundown sheet information in the far left column. Allow about 3″ or 4″ for each scene to make sure there is enough room for complete entries in the other six columns. Allow extra space for particularly large scenes with several musical numbers.

The second column of the production guide deals with the setting. Next to each scene briefly describe the set, subject and type of set piece, i.e., drop, scrim, revolving set, etc. Also, list stage position of any set item if it is particularly important. Make sure all entries fit within your production limitations.

Proceed to the next column, which lists the lighting requirements and changes within the scene. When notes on the set and lighting have been posted, proceed through each function, adding pertinent details to each scene as you go. For example, costumes: Will there be any costume changes; how many costumes will be required for the scene; will any special costumes be required? The number of people in the scene: Are they on stage at the rise or do they enter? What does the stage crew do during this scene? Are there any special effects? (Theoretically a property list should be included in this type of planning, but including it at this stage is not necessary. A prop list to fit each scene should be prepared by the prop master during the preproduction meetings.)

The most important column is the change-of-scene column. This entry tells exactly how the action proceeds to the next scene; i.e., drop flies, set revolves, lights cross fade, blackout, curtain, etc. It's this column that ties the production guide together and allows the production staff to estimate running time, production materials, and personnel requirements. It avoids such problems as cutting out an extraneous scene only to find later that it was necessary to provide enough time to make a set change.

PRODUCTION GUIDE "THE MUSIC MAN" (Figure 3-2)

THE MUSIC MAN ACT I	SETS	LIGHTING	COSTUMES	NUMBER OF PEOPLE IN SCENE	CHANGE OF SCENE	BACK STAGE ACTION
OVERTURE	Main curtain up on orchestra drop. Title on big base drum plus other musical instruments.	Colorful lighting. White light singles out drum with title.	—	—	Drop flies to reveal locomotive drop.	Everyone ready for Railway Coach Scene One.
Last 24 bars of OVERTURE	Speeding locomotive (1912 Type) scrim.	Hold color, take out drum lighting as orchestra drop flies out.			CO_2 equipment detaches, scrim dissolves to reveal Railway Coach.	Full stage in use. Ready Iowa town behind Railway Coach. Special steam effect, CO_2 billows from smokestack and streaks from wheel.
ACT I— SCENE I						
The morning of July 4, 1912, on a train somewhere in Iowa "ROCK ISLAND"	Railway Coach	Lights on coach only.	Business suits of time. Conductor uniform of time. Harold has reversible jacket that converts to drum major uniform.	8 Traveling Salesmen Harold Hill Conductor	Coach splits in two and off revealing River City's main street.	Lights streaking by in coach windows. Salesmen bounce as if on train. Full stage in use.
ACT I— SCENE II						
River City, Iowa, center of town. Immediately following, townspeople standing in tableau sing "IOWA STUBBORN"	Town Square, Buildings, Church, Billiard Parlor with name in full view.	Exterior lighting.	1912 work clothes, suits, skirts, petticoats, etc.	Townfolk, Sing Chorus, Dance Chorus Kids, Harold Hill, Washburn enters after number.	—	Full stage in use. Ready street drop and/or traveler Paroo porch.
"TROUBLE"	Same	Follow spot on Harold Hill.	Same	Same Marian enters.	Residential street. Scrim drop or painted scrim traveler comes in.	Street in one. Move house into position in 30 seconds.
ACT I— SCENE III						
Residential street. Porch of Paroo House. House interior that evening. "PIANO LESSON"	Scrim drop or traveler, then porch on wagon stage left in front of scrim, then Paroo house.	Evening. Exterior lighting on scrim, then stage spot on porch, then lights up on house interior. Fore stage lights fade.	Same	Marian, Harold Hill, then Mrs. Paroo, Amaryllis	Scrim flies as lights on house interior reach full.	Full stage in use. Ready to strike house, and fly in gym, and remove porch at the end of "Goodnight My Someone."
"GOODNIGHT MY SOMEONE"	Same	Follow spot on Marian.	Same	Marian	During song Marian crosses to porch where she concludes number as house is struck and gym flies in during dimout of follow spot.	Gym platforms and wagons move in.

PRODUCTION GUIDE (*continued*)

THE MUSIC MAN ACT I	SETS	LIGHTING	COSTUMES	NUMBER OF PEOPLE IN SCENE	CHANGE OF SCENE	BACK STAGE ACTION
ACT I— SCENE IV Interior of the Madison Gymnasium, River City High School. Thirty minutes later. "SEVENTY-SIX TROMBONES" "SINCERE"	Gym backdrop. Side legs of July 4th bunting and gym equipment. Ceiling borders with suspended gym lights. Platform, speakers' rostrum, and folding chairs	General interior lighting. Follow spot on Harold Hill for song. Follow spot on School Board members for song.	Columbia costume. Dress-up wear of 1912. Historical costumes for performing groups.	Mrs. Shinn, Townspeople, Kids, Mayor Shinn, School Board members. Entering scene: Marian, Harold, Tommy.	Scrim and library exterior fly in as Harold Hill and Marian exit.	Full stage in use. Ready to fly in residential scrim and library insert (exterior). Strike gym platforms and fly drops and legs.
ACT I— SCENE V Street in front of the library immediately following.	Residential traveler used in Scene III. Insert set piece of Madison Public Library. (Front doors should open)	Evening Exterior Street Lights Light blue and amber stage spots for moonlight.	Same	All entering scene: Harold Hill, Marian, Washburn, Principal and Chorus ladies of River City School Board.	—	Scene played in one. Strike gym and set up library interior.
"THE SADDER-BUT-WISER GIRL" (soft shoe)	Same	Same plus follow spots on Hill and Washburn during number.	Same	Harold Hill, Washburn.	—	Ready to fly scrim and library exterior.
"PICKALITTLE"	Same	Follow spot on Harold Hill. Stage spots on ladies.	Same	Harold Hill, Ladies.		
"GOODNIGHT LADIES"	Same	Same	Same	School Board sing counterpoint to "PICKALITTLE"	BLACKOUT: Library exterior flies. Lights up on library interior, scrim flies as lighting near full.	Ready to return same scene at conclusion of next scene.
ACT I— SCENE VI Interior of Madison Library immediately following "MARIAN THE LIBRARIAN"	Staggered sections of book shelves. Checkout desk. Two reading tables with benches.	Interior lighting. Illuminated chandelier.	—	Harold Hill, Marian, Boy and Girl Dance Chorus.	BLACKOUT: Library exterior and residential street scrim fly in.	Strike Library and set up River City main street as in Act I, Scene II. Ready to fly library exterior and move in Paroo porch.
ACT I— SCENE VII Exterior on library. The following Saturday noon.	Same as Act I, Scene V.	Bright exterior.	Back to street clothes.	Harold Hill, Tommy, Mayor Shinn.	BLACKOUT: Fly library exterior only. Move in Paroo porch.	Ready to fly scrim and to strike Paroo porch.

PRODUCTION GUIDE (*continued*)

THE MUSIC MAN ACT I	SETS	LIGHTING	COSTUMES	NUMBER OF PEOPLE IN SCENE	CHANGE OF SCENE	BACK STAGE ACTION
ACT I—SCENE VIII The Paroo porch that evening	Same as the beginning of Act I, Scene III.	Evening.	—	Mrs. Paroo, Winthrop, Harold Hill.	Dimout as song ends. Porch slides out, scrim flies to reveal center of town.	Cast moves into set as it is completed.
"MY WHITE KNIGHT"		Follow spot on Marian as she sings.	Marian has different dress.	Marian enters.		Ready main curtain.
ACT I—SCENE IX Center of town. Noon, the following Saturday.	Same as Act I, Scene II.	General daylight exterior lighting.	Same	Winthrop, Townsfolk.		
"WELLS FARGO WAGON"	Wells Fargo wagon (with horse, if possible).	Follow spot on Winthrop as he sings.		Eventually everyone enters and sings.		Set up Gym during intermission.

CURTAIN

THE MUSIC MAN ACT II	SETS	LIGHTING	COSTUMES	NUMBER OF PEOPLE IN SCENE	CHANGE OF SCENE	BACK STAGE ACTION
ACT II—SCENE I Madison Gymnasium. The following Tuesday evening. "IT'S YOU"	Curtain up on same as Act I, Scene IV.	General interior lighting.	Ladies Auxiliary in bloomer outfits. School Board in Indian costumes. Informal evening dress of the 1912 period.	All but smaller children.	—	Full stage in use.
"SHIPOOPI" (Song and Dance)	Same	Follow spot on Marcellus through first chorus of song.	Same	Same	—	Ready to blackout and fly in street scrim and hotel.
"PICKALITTLE" Reprise.	Same	General interior	Same	Ladies Auxiliary, Marian, Harold Hill.	Blackout, fly in street scrim and hotel insert set.	Ready to move on Paroo porch.
ACT II—SCENE II The Hotel porch Wednesday evening, after supper. "LIDA ROSE"	Scrim as used in Act I, Scene III Hotel insert, front section with name, hotel door should open.	Lights up on Hotel only.	School Board now in street wear.	School Board. Harold enters and exits as singing starts.	—	Strike Gym. Ready to remove Hotel.

PRODUCTION GUIDE (*continued*)

THE MUSIC MAN ACT II	SETS	LIGHTING	COSTUMES	NUMBER OF PEOPLE IN SCENE	CHANGE OF SCENE	BACK STAGE ACTION
The Paroo porch. "WILL I EVER TELL YOU"	Paroo porch is pushed on as "Lida Rose" gets underway.	Lights cross fade to ½ as follow spot hits Marian when she takes over with her song.	Marian has different dress.	Marian comes on with Paroo porch.	Lights fade completely on School Board as song ends. Hotel goes out on applause.	
ACT II— SCENE III The Paroo porch. Immediately following.	Remaining from previous Scene.	Lights up on porch plus general night lighting on scrim.	Same	Mrs. Paroo, Marian, Winthrop enters.	—	Set up Footbridge scene. Ready to strike porch and fly scrim.
"GARY, INDIANA"	Same	Follow spot on Winthrop during song.	Same	Charlie enters. School Board enters and exits with Charlie. Harold enters.	Blackout. Remove porch and fly scrim to reveal Footbridge.	Ready to return scrim.
ACT II— SCENE IV The Footbridge, 15 minutes later "IT'S YOU" Reprise.	Sky drop. Ground row set legs and borders of trees and foliage. Footbridge spanning about 8 feet.	Backdrop light giving silhouette effect of set and people on their way to the Social.	Go-to-meeting clothes.	Townspeople. Boy and Girl Dance Chorus. Marian and Harold enter.	—	Set up assembly room (Possible: Gym converted to Meeting Hall) Ready park bench and lamppost.
"TILL THERE WAS YOU"	Same	Follow spots on Marian and Harold Hill.	Same	Marian, Harold.	Street scrim flies in.	Ready to push park set on.
ACT II— SCENE V A street. Immediately following.	Scrim as used in Act I, Scene III.	Evening.	Same	Harold Hill.	BLACKOUT. Park bench and lamppost are pushed on.	
"SEVENTY-SIX TROMBONES" and "GOOD-NIGHT MY SOMEONE"		Blue spot on Harold Hill.		Charlie, Marcellus enter.		Ready to fly scrim and strike park set.
ACT II— SCENE VI Madison Park, a few minutes later.	Same as preceding, with park bench and lamppost.	Same general evening lighting at start, then stage spot lighting on area of group.	Same	Townspeople move through scene as Charlie reveals Harold Hill's past. They pass as Harold Hill, Marian enter behind Winthrop.	Fly curtain as park set is being struck	
ACT II— SCENE VII River City High School Assembly Room, immediately following.	Separate set or Gymnasium converted to Meeting Hall.	General interior.	Children in band uniforms	Entire cast.	CURTAIN.	Ready for final curtain calls.

There are many more benefits to preparing the production guide. It forces the director to learn much more about his show than he normally would this early in the game. It makes budgeting a lot easier and provides a composite picture from which it is easy to eliminate costumes and production "frills," should the budget demand it. The stage manager's cues are ready for posting. But most of all, it leaves no doubt about what is to be done. The jobs are clear-cut. No one can say, "I didn't know what was expected of me." All these important elements get done when you can say, "Here it is. Create it!"

When the production guide is completed the job of doing the musical is clearly defined. All that remains to preplanning is the task of scheduling each function. This involves planning the rehearsal schedule and setting deadlines by which time each function must be completed.

THE PRODUCTION SCHEDULE

Avid mystery book readers would never read the ending first. They toil through the most routine plots, carefully judging the evidence and deciding for themselves who's the guilty party. The mystery writer works in reverse. He decides on a good ending and then builds his plot and subplots.

When producing a musical, the production staff must function like the mystery writer and the mystery reader at the same time. They must know the ending and everything that comes before so they can then build their production to a successful ending.

The production staff, acting as the mystery writer, must back-date to the opening night in order to "plot" the production schedule. Once plotted, they must avidly "read" their singers, dancers, and actors back through the production schedule to the ending, the final curtain of the last performance.

The production schedule is a valuable tool in many respects, but there is one particular job it does best. That is *to remove the commonly held theatrical dogma that the only real deadline is opening night.* People will knock themselves out the night before opening night because they've "got to get the show there." Why not knock themselves out a week before? Then all the elements would "be there" for everybody to get used to them. If a group can make an opening night deadline, they can make an earlier deadline and have a better production. When the job is clearly outlined in the beginning, the only problem in meeting the deadline is to allow enough time.

Correct allocation of time comes with experience. To be safe in first attempts, plan extra time. Working five nights a week, the following are safe guidelines: For making sets and costumes, plan on about eight to ten weeks; blocking the direction, about seven weeks; chorus numbers, five weeks; setting dance numbers, eight weeks; collection of props, about four weeks; hanging the sets, about one week. With a few musical productions under the group's belt, these times can be reduced somewhat, and, of course, a lot depends on the size of the production.

Planning the production schedule starts with closing night. It includes all the calendar days from the first day of casting through the final performance. It establishes deadlines for each step of production and maps out a practical rehearsal schedule. It is an important tool in gauging how much time will be required to do the job right. It also provides a good check for determining if work is progressing on schedule or where time is being wasted.

PREPARING THE PRODUCTION SCHEDULE

When the production dates have been set, and the time estimates for each function have been figured, it is time to plot the production schedule. Using the calculated times, plot each function from its deadline back to the point at which each function should get underway. When each function has been plotted, the entire production objective is broken down into daily goals that are realistic, that result in a heads-up production, and eliminate wasted time.

Prepare the production schedule on an 8½" x 11" "month-at-a-glance" calendar pad, which is available at any office supply or stationery store. (If you wish to draw your own squares and fill in the dates, ordinary paper will do just as well.)

The sample production schedule (Figure 3-3) called for nine full weeks from casting to performance. Rehearsal times were scheduled in the evening during the week, plus a few Saturday and Sunday afternoons. This schedule can be altered to fit production conditions. A Cleveland high-school director writes:

Because of the size of this educational venture we spread our production over a three-month period. The first week is devoted to auditions which usually runs about 600 students. The second to the ninth week are spent in individual rehearsals once a week on Sunday afternoons. The chorus is taken by our choral director, the dancers by the

Carnival *as produced by J. S. Morton High School, Cicero, Illinois, directed by Jack L. Leckel.*

MONDAY	TUESDAY	WEDNESDAY	THURSDAY	FRIDAY	SATURDAY	SUNDAY
February 1 Casting	2 Casting	3 Casting for final selection	4 Post Cast Cast read through entire show and sing part of each song 7:30 P.M. Measurements for <u>Costumes</u>	5 Off D: Director C: Choreographer M: Musical Director Rehearsals Held In Separate Locations	6 Off	7 Off
8 D: Act I, Scene 5 Dialogue only C: Dance Chorus "Embassy Waltz" M: Sing Chorus 7:30-10:00 Learn numbers	9 D: Act I Scenes 2,4,6 Dialogue only C: Dance Chorus "Embassy Waltz" M: Sing Chorus 7:30-10:00 Learn numbers	10 D: Act I, Scene 3 Dialogue only C: Dance Chorus "Embassy Waltz" M: Sing Chorus 7:30-10:00 Learn numbers	11 D: Act I, Scene 7 Dialogue only C: Dance Chorus "Embassy Waltz" and Act I, Scene 11 M: Sing Chorus 7:30-10:00 Learn numbers	12 D: Block "I'm An Ordinary Man" C: "Wouldn't It Be Loverly?" M: "Little Bit of Luck", Principals only	13 Off	14 Off
15 D: Act I Scenes 9,10 C: Sing and Dance Chorus "Ascot Gavotte" M: "Ascot Gavotte"	16 D: Act I, Scene 8 then join choreographer C: Sing and Dance Chorus "Ascot Gavotte" with principals and dialogue M: "Ascot Gavotte"	17 D: Act I, Scene 1 "Why Can't the English?" C: "Little Bit of Luck" M: "On the Street Where You Live"	18 D: "On the Street Where You Live" C: "The Rain in Spain" M: Choral Work in Act I, Scene 5 "Poor Professor Higgins!"	19 Liza - D: "Just You Wait" C: "I Could Have" M: Danced All Night"	20 Individual singing rehearsals for leads (afternoon)	21 Run through Act I, as ragged as it may be. Stop to correct blocking difficulties <u>Scripts Permitted</u>
22 Run through and correct Act I, Scenes 1-5	23 Run through and correct Act I, Scenes 6-11 Act I Songs - <u>Memorized</u>	24 D: Act II, Scene 5 Dialogue only C: "Get Me to the Church on Time" M: <u>First Orchestra Reading</u>	25 D: Act II, Scene 6 "I've Grown Accustomed to Her Face" Then Act II, Scene 7 C: Act II, Scene 2 "Show Me" M: Off	26 Off-or reserved for trouble spots	27 Individual singing rehearsals for leads (afternoon)	28 Run through Act I No Scripts
March 1 D: Act II, Scene 3 C: Work everything together M: Chorus rehearsal	2 D: Act II, Scene 4 C: "Embassy Waltz" "Ascot Gavotte" Chorus only M: "Show Me"	3 D: Act II, Scene 1 C: "You Did It" M: Orchestra rehearsal	4 D: Complete C: unfinished M: blocking for Acts I or II	5 Off-or reserved for trouble spots	6 Individual Singing rehearsals for leads (Afternoon)	7 Run through Act II Stop to correct blocking difficulties <u>Scripts Permitted</u>

MONDAY	TUESDAY	WEDNESDAY	THURSDAY	FRIDAY	SATURDAY	SUNDAY
8 March (Cont.) Run through and correct trouble spots in Act II	**9** Use as necessary	**10** Run through Act II No Scripts M: Orchestra rehearsal	**11** Run through Act I No Scripts First Costume Fitting (If costumes are being made)	**12** Use as necessary	**13** Afternoon Singing Rehearsal (Optional)	**14** Run through Act I and Act II
15 Fix trouble spots in Act I	**16** Fix trouble spots in Act I	**17** Fix trouble spots in Act II M: Orchestra rehearsal	**18** Fix trouble spots in Act II	**19** Big Social Event of Year -- No Rehearsal	**20** Off	**21** Complete run through No Scripts All Props Required and Orchestra Joins Cast
22 Polish Act I, Scenes 1-8 with orchestra	**23** Polish Act I, Scenes 9-11 and Act II with orchestra	**24** All Sets Completed and Erected Run through Act I with stops for corrections -- no orchestra	**25** Costumes Received or Completed Act II with stops for corrections -- no orchestra	**26** Cast off except for numbers requiring special attention. No orchestra Make set adjustments	**27** Afternoon Singing Rehearsal (Optional) All Lighting Complete	**28** Full Dress Rehearsal Complete Show - No Stops Make-up call 1:15 p.m. Pictures
29 Polish Act I Run through No stops --- Go back and make the necessary corrections	**30** Polish Act II Run through No stops --- Go back through and make necessary corrections	**31** Full Dress Rehearsal 6:00 No Make-Up	**1** April Polish necessary numbers only Final technical adjustments	**2** Performance 8:30 P.M.	**3** Performance 8:30 P.M.	**4** Performance 8:00 P.M.
5 Off	**6** Off	**7** Off	**8** Brush-up Run through No Costumes	**9** Performance 8:30 P.M.	**10** Performance 8:30 P.M.	**11** Performance 8:00 P.M.

choreographers, and I take the actors and actresses. After rehearsal I rehearse the soloists and small quartets, if any. I attend the dance rehearsals which are Sunday evenings from 7 P.M. to 9 P.M., but no other rehearsals.

The stage crew works on the sets on Saturday mornings. (You will note that I use separate groups for the dancing and singing choruses and later on I interweave them.) The orchestra rehearses separately from the 5th to the 9th week under the direction of our instrumental director. We rehearse all together from the 10th to the 12th week at which time all music is under the direction of the instrumental director.

We have three rehearsals a week during the 10th and 11th weeks and we rehearse every day during the 12th week. It is during this week that the production crews come to rehearsals and we use all the scenery. Thursday of this week is our dress rehearsal and we open on Friday night.

Incidentally, during our dress rehearsal we invite the parents of the cast. This gives them an opportunity to take pictures since this is not permitted on the show nights themselves, and it also gives the cast a chance to react to laughter and applause.

Another high school spreads its production over a similar span of time, but holds cast rehearsals in the afternoon, right after the close of the regular school day. Their orchestra practices during school time as part of the music department's curriculum. The last three weeks are spent with the entire cast and orchestra in evening rehearsals.

SIDELIGHTS

Individual production staff members may find it handy to copy information and deadlines dealing with their function from the master production schedule. The director and/or stage manager should make it a practice to check with each staff member about three to five days prior to deadline dates to make sure each phase will be completed on time.

The sample production schedule lists per-formances on two succeeding weekends. This performance plan has some important advantages: 1) If the show is good, word of mouth will sell lots of extra tickets for the second week. 2) More people prefer to attend theatre on weekends. 3) People busy one week will have a chance to attend the other. 4) The performers' memorable experience of being in the musical isn't over all at once. Possible disadvantages include: extra payment on rented costumes and materials; a lean second weekend if the show is bad; and production conflicts for busy theatres.

Weekdays are inconvenient and may result in some thin audiences. This is not only bad business but can hurt the players' morale. And in this author's judgment, producing a musical for only two or three performances is not worthwhile; let alone the inconsideration for the people who have invested hundreds of hours of time.

Creative people tend to dislike scheduling and paper work organization. They will like this system as it is part of the creative process and sparks new ideas and approaches to the *whole* objective. It also makes them look better because it allows them to reach their full creative capacity and to show off a superior production.

The production guide and the production schedule are easy to prepare. The total time to prepare them for a large musical may take from ten to twenty hours, but they require decisions that must be made anyway. They cover important points that can be conquered long before casting or rehearsals ever get started. They will save countless hours and mistakes later on.

It's not the time it takes to put the production together that makes a successful musical, it's the time spent putting all the parts together and polishing the whole under actual production conditions. Organized preplanning is the most efficient and surest means to this end.

It cannot be reiterated often enough: Producing a nonprofessional musical is a group effort. Preplanning and harmonious team work are the most essential keys to success.

CHAPTER IV The Director and Stage Manager

*"The One Most Likely to Make
the Show Succeed"*

There is no way to succeed in directing without really trying. A new "old Chinese proverb" might state: "Anyone who undertakes the task of presenting a musical show must have the mouth of Confucius, the patience of a saint, the cunning of a lion—and at least half the brains to match."

THE DIRECTOR'S SCOPE OF OPERATION

The first thing the director is interested in is the selection of the musical. In some groups the selection is made by a play-reading group, student committee, or a popular vote of group members. Although these are fine democratic methods, a director might get stuck with a show he doesn't want to do. And if the director isn't interested in the chosen show, he might as well give up right there.

The responsibilities of the director of a musical increase in relation to the added functions of music and dance and the increased size of cast and production. Basically his duties break down into six main areas:

1) Planning
2) Scheduling
3) Casting
4) Stage direction or blocking
5) Character development
6) Connecting

The director must plan so well that he can talk about any part of the show with full understanding and confidence. Then using the procedure outlined in Chapter III he must work with the production staff to develop a production plan on which everyone can agree. As creative and organization head of the production staff, the director must delegate work to the other specifically skilled staff members. They should know what the director wants and, unless otherwise requested, be left alone to achieve the proper results. Periodic checks should be made by the director to make sure they are meeting the production schedule and that they are producing results within the production style and guidelines set down in the preproduction meetings. If things are not running on schedule, help should be brought in immediately and extra work sessions planned to make up the lost time.

Casting, stage direction, and character development present new problems in musical productions and these will be mentioned throughout the chapter. A unique problem, however, is the connection of all the various songs, dances, and scenes into a smooth-running show.

UNDERSTANDING THE MUSICAL BOOK

The play or "book" part of a musical is the director's main chore. In a straight play, the curtain goes up and the action moves uninterrupted to the intermission curtain; then again after intermission to the end of the show. Drama, comedy, or mystery, a play is a whole in itself, a single unit and form of theatrical expression.

The *whole* of a musical, on the other hand, is made up of many parts and various forms of theatrical and musical expression. Singing, dancing, acting, and sometimes just the change of scenery are individual parts. In a play there is only the action to direct. In a musical the transition from part to part becomes vital to, and part of, the action. By making up the production guide and production schedule, as described in Chapter III, it becomes easy to break the whole down into parts and confidently to reassemble the *whole* for run-throughs, dress rehearsal, and performance. The importance of any given part depends on how the musical is "constructed."

In writing of modern musical comedies the emphasis is on "construction."

As was mentioned briefly before, construction is the integration of book, music, lyrics, dances, and movement of the production. In theory, each line, song, dance, or movement advances the show rather than stopping the story progression for mere entertainment. Unfortunately, few musicals maintain the theory throughout, but every successful show of recent times was written with the tightest possible construction in mind.

In tightly constructed musicals the action moves naturally from drama to song to dance to drama, part to part, scene change to scene change. The most difficult parts are easily recognized. Weaknesses written into loosely constructed musicals may not seem difficult on paper, but once on the stage the scene (or part) falls flat.

For example, most writers of musicals written in the 1940's and early 1950's believed that all set changes should be hidden from the audience. The musicals of the time had a "show" curtain: a drop carrying out the theme of the show used to cover a scene change whenever there wasn't a better way to do it. Usually a short gag scene or run-through action was inserted to keep things moving. Sometimes the orchestra simply played an interlude

of music. Since this completely stopped the plot progression, new techniques were developed to eliminate these dead spots.

Due to modern scene-changing methods, such scenes are no longer necessary. They can be cut from shows that have them without damage. Even if the scenes remain, they can be played out front without the extra drop.

Whenever a director can make the parts of his musical flow together more smoothly he improves the construction and betters his production.

The important fact is to recognize tight or loose spots, or violations of the construction theory and then direct accordingly. Where the construction is tight (the transfer from dialogue to song to dance is smooth and natural), the direction must be tight. Long stage crosses, unnecessary time for a line or music cue, or the insertion of extra bits of business contradict the writing achievement and are detrimental to the show.

One of the best examples of tight construc-

Beverly Liebenstein directed this production of L'il Abner *at Kellogg High School, St. Paul, Minnesota.*

tion is *My Fair Lady*. Everything moves naturally from one scene to another. Every line, song, and dance in this unlikely adaptation of G. B. Shaw's *Pygmalion* tells the audience something new. The show never stops to put on the latest dance steps or to prove the author's wit on current affairs. (Not that the shows that do so aren't any good, but when they do, they weaken their construction.)

Mechanical set movement played an important part in the Broadway production of *My Fair Lady*. Since that time, mechanical stages have become quite common and have done a major service in covering a lot of poor construction.

If nonprofessionals cannot provide this type of flexible settings, thought should be given to other means that take up the slack. Some solutions might be: partial sets instead of full stage settings; projected settings; moving the action out of the set before it has ended and changing scenes in darkness; working the scene or number downstage in tightly controlled lighting (from above, sides, or high spot); or any other directing effort to keep the show moving at a rapid pace. In a tightly constructed show, never wait for the applause to die down. Maintain the proper pace by moving right into the next part. If the audience stops the show, freeze the action until play can be resumed. It's bad for nonprofessionals to "milk" the audience (encourage applause), particularly in a tight show.

The best example of a loosely constructed musical is the revue or variety show. This is an extreme example; one in which the parts are completely unrelated, except for the fact that they are all parts of the same show. *Oklahoma!, Irma La Douce, The Boy Friend, Stop the World–I Want to Get Off,* and *Anything Goes* are all loosely constructed musicals. *Oklahoma!* succeeded on innovation and a great score. *Irma La Douce* jokes from one musical or dance number to another (to tighten construction, the movie version was done as a play). *The Boy Friend* has virtually nothing to hold it together other than strong satire. *Stop the World–I Want to Get Off* covers its loose construction with style. *Anything Goes* is an album of old-time hit songs and slapstick fun. Each of these shows was a hit in its own time. Some succeeded when good construction didn't mean as much as it does to modern musicals; others disregarded the principles of construction to accomplish what they set out to do. Recognizing the role of construction in the musical your group has selected is the key to the whole production.

Unfortunately, there are more loosely constructed musicals than tightly constructed ones, so there is plenty of room for a good director and his production staff to tighten things up. To do so, the staff must take the attitude on how the show can be done *better,* not just how the show can be done, period. Broadway is always experimenting with new ideas. These are not completely without fault. Reference to material of the Broadway production is a great source to the nonprofessional production, but it should be looked upon as a starting point, not the answer (particularly in loosely constructed musicals).

Another way to improve loosely constructed musicals is by cutting extraneous material. Some groups make a regular practice of shortening the running time regardless of construction. Usually this can be done without difficulty. Broadway musicals are usually tailored to run 2½ hours, including a 15-minute intermission. A nonprofessional group performing the same show would probably run 2 hours and 45 minutes, which can be tiring on the audience. All but the most tightly constructed musicals can stand some cutting.

Examples of loose construction and potential improvements in the nonprofessional production would fill another book, but a few pointers to keep in mind are: 1) anything that does not advance the beginning to the end, or help to establish a character, is a filler that usually requires strong direction (strong enough that the sequence could stand by itself). If such fillers cannot carry their own and tend to drag the nonprofessional production, they should be eliminated; 2) it is senseless to add any additional material that does not fit within the construction of the musical or to change extraneous material to fit local audiences. This author has observed some ghastly changes in two wonderful works. In a production of *Guys and Dolls* the director interpreted the "Luck Be a Lady" number as Lady Luck hovering over a bunch of spellbound gamblers and cast his wife in an unimpressive ballet sequence that robbed the audience of the emotional explosion of professional crapshooters gambling with their very souls. The second incident was a production of *Carnival* in which a local magician saw a chance to destroy a masterpiece of construction with a trunkful of stale magic tricks.

There have been many others, but these two examples are most pointed. The real tragedy is that these particular groups thought these changes were an improvement, whereas, in fact, they degraded their production.

Sometimes the authors violate their own story lines or twist scenes in an illogical sequence. These "holes" in the plot sometimes weaken the show, but always offer the director an opportunity for improvement. Because the authors must weave so many numbers, characters, scenes, etc., into a musical in a relatively short time, plus the fact that changes are made in the hectic pre-Broadway period, it is almost impossible to pick up all the loose ends. Once opening night is achieved, the show is usually "frozen" and no more changes are made.

ONE EXAMPLE OF PICKING UP LOOSE ENDS

Little Mary Sunshine is a wonderful spoof of the operettas of old. In the second act, our hero, Captain Jim, readies himself to capture a desperate Indian renegade named Yellow Feather. Before entering the woods alone, he tells Corporal Billy Jester of his dangerous mission and orders him to come in after him

if he is not back by 9 o'clock. Promptly Billy passes an order for the remaining forest rangers to follow him if he doesn't return. When learning of Billy's orders, his girl friend, Nancy, also departs on the hunt for Yellow Feather.

As written, only Billy, Nancy, and Yellow Feather cross paths in the woods. They tiptoe around the woods for several minutes and make like shadows of one another—a melodramatic technique used in many early 20th-century operettas and movies. (The "Shell Game" number.) The next reference to Nancy, Billy, plus Captain Jim and the remaining forest rangers is near the finale, when they are all seen returning from the woods. (Little Mary's line: "Look, Captain Jim, your brave men return.")

There we have a violation or hole in the story line because Captain Jim and the forest rangers are not seen in the woods with Yellow Feather. Captain Jim later captures Yellow Feather near Little Mary's Inn (not in the

Scenes from Little Mary Sunshine, *directed by Gale A. Toraason at Aurora West Senior High School, Aurora, Illinois. Stylized direction is an absolute must for shows of this nature. Extra research can really pay off—in this case a study of the old operettas that inspired this outrageous spoof.*

woods) and the forest rangers come marching out of the woods for the finale. They were never seen entering the woods or taking part in any action in the woods.

The melodramatic technique is good, but could be changed a little with some interesting results. One presentation worked out thus: the music for the "Shell Game" was shifted around a little (six bars of thunderous music were assigned to the forest rangers as a theme whenever they crossed the scene, and some other repeats in the music were added or deleted as necessary). The number started with Yellow Feather and a weary Captain Jim passing within inches of each other in their search. Enter Billy and Nancy in turn (theme music for each already supplied in "Shell Game" score). Each just misses Yellow Feather and Captain Jim. After each enters and pauses to listen, the herd of forest rangers (to their theme music) steals across the stage unnoticed in exaggerated tiptoe motion. Captain Jim gives up and returns in the direction of the Inn. Billy and Nancy run into each other and proceed together. Again they just miss Yellow Feather and go unnoticed in their search. All stop and strain for pause while the rangers make another complete cross, still undetected. Then Billy and Nancy cross down to the corner of the stage as Yellow Feather spots the forest rangers. Seeing that there are too many, he hides on the audience side of a large tree up stage center and waits for the troops to pass behind the tree. Instead of passing behind, the eight forest rangers disappear behind the foot-wide tree. The stunned Yellow Feather circles the tree to no avail. After a quick take to the audience he starts around again, but is chased back by the eight rangers, who come thundering from behind the thin tree. In pursuit the rangers run smack dab into Billy and Nancy, who make it a joint effort. Soon Yellow Feather is surrounded. The circle closes in until everyone except Nancy jumps on Yellow Feather. Everyone is up quickly, but all that remains is Yellow Feather's Indian suit and a bright yellow feather. Yellow Feather's impossible escape is established, and the scene blacks out.

The imaginative effects were accomplished by two swinging inserts in the ground row background and a breakaway Indian costume. Yellow Feather was underdressed as a forest ranger. His Indian wig was quickly stashed in one of the regular ranger's hats during the pileup. When Yellow Feather disappeared, no one realized that another ranger (without a hat and with war paint) had been added.

A violation in construction was plugged with added entertainment value to the audience. The action fulfilled what the plot had designed. The nonprofessional director turned a liability (of an outdated technique and a hole in the construction) into an asset.

Another example was the off-Broadway revival of Cole Porter's *Anything Goes*. This production used Porter hits from other shows to replace weak numbers in the original score. There are a lot of low-royalty, older (and loosely constructed) shows that would provide fresh entertainment and plenty of hit songs if similarly adapted.

A change in the original concept, updated jokes, insertion of local material carefully fitted into the construction of the show are just a few of the ways the nonprofessional director can take a loosely constructed musical apart and put together a hit.

The general rule in altering construction is to: 1) know the show completely; 2) judge the construction with great care; 3) avoid tampering with tightly constructed shows; 4) make sure the alterations to loose construction make the musical tighter.

Handling Personnel for Musicals

The director of amateur players has a much more difficult task than a director of professional actors. Professional actors maintain silence and poise, they respond well to direction, and help the director achieve the desired effect. Nonprofessionals tend to socialize, erroneously interpret their own parts, and reject the drilling needed to achieve the quality production worthy of paid admissions.

Getting a giant-size cast of nonprofessionals to produce their best effort is a difficult task; mainly because they don't understand what it is. The two main points to keep in mind are:

1) to provide basic training and
2) to instill confidence in themselves as actors and in you as their director.

Bridge is a difficult card game. People find it difficult to learn by watching other people play, and often take lessons. There was one highly successful teacher of basic bridge who always started each new group of pupils by saying, "This is a bridge deck. There are fifty-two cards. This is how we deal the cards." And so he went, sparing no details. People rarely dropped out of his classes, and he could never accommodate all the people who wished to learn from him.

This bridge teacher enjoyed success because the people he taught played good bridge. Everybody in his classes learned to be good bridge players because he told them everything *necessary* to become a good bridge player. He knew that you can't make *any* assumptions about what people know or what they don't know. The only way to be sure they will perform the way you want them to is to tell them *exactly* what to do. Too many people won't say what they don't know or understand. They must be shown.

The nonprofessional needs stronger and more detailed direction. He tends to be immature on stage and is prone to overact or to mug things he thinks should be funny. Always explain the basics and the reason for the action. Show exactly what to do with hands and feet. Most nonprofessionals must have this type of information but seldom will ask for it. *Never expect any results on stage you didn't communicate to the cast in rehearsals.* If there is a chance for misunderstanding, someone *will* misunderstand. For example: With so many high schools doing musicals, more help should be aimed at the proper interpretation of adult roles. As adult-"watchers," they think they know how an adult should act. Most do not. Even if they did, it would probably be a mimic of *an adult* and not the character of the role. The main factor is that they don't understand the way the character would act. If this is explained to each principal actor, along with 15 minutes to a half hour of private drill with the director to insure the correct understanding of the character *before* rehearsals begin, it will mean a world of difference to the overall success of the show.

When nonprofessionals know their director is with them all the way, they will knock themselves out to please him. The only way he will have time for this personal service is to have his show well planned and a production staff that does its part.

Plan and block rehearsals in advance. Once started, run through scenes over and over again. It's the best way to build confidence: confidence in a line, confidence in stage moves, confidence in the music, confidence in the other members of the cast. The confidence that is absolutely necessary in building a successful show—the kind of show that will make the audience sit up and take notice.

Another big help is to have the actors learn their lines and songs before rehearsals get under way. There is some danger of their forming some wrong concepts this way, but the time gained is a tremendous advantage.

Musicals are built line by line, part by part. Often a part directed one way will need to be changed because it doesn't work. Unfortunately, nonprofessionals tend to resist direction changes when a scene or number doesn't work. Such changes can rattle their confidence, particularly if made in the last week of production. The way most nonprofessional musicals come down to the wire, such last-minute changes are virtually impossible. Yet it is a waste to present something that is obviously wrong when a few simple changes could make the picture much brighter. It's just one more reason for a production schedule with plenty of room for changes and brush-up rehearsals.

One of the most admirable qualities any director can possess is the ability to judge his own work objectively and make necessary improvements. The trick is to have the confidence of the cast so they will accept changes as the normal course of events.

This is where director "salesmanship" comes in. The director must win the confidence of his cast so they will follow his direction, knowing that it is the best and only thing to do. He should be friendly, but not become buddy-buddy to the point that some cast members assume special privileges and reduce their effort. The director must always maintain the upper hand, but never adopt regimentation in lieu of creative instruction.

Set down the rules at the time of tryouts and enforce them even if it means replacement of an uncooperative cast member. Wasted time results in a weakened show. With the bigness of musical productions, punctuality at rehearsals, meeting deadlines, independent initiative, cast care of costumes, etc., become even bigger factors for a smooth-running show. Participants who cannot accept simple discipline can only hurt the production.

Nonprofessionals need *definite* instructions on what to do when the audience stops the show. Don't leave anything to the cast or production crews' judgment. If a particular number is a show-stopper, plan for it. Build an encore into the production plan as an option. If it happens, everyone is prepared; if no action is stopped, everyone is ready to go right into the next bit. This will eliminate amateur ad-libs, departures from character, and general confusion that may drag the show or ruin the following action. And if the audience is cut a little short, all the better. It never hurts to leave them wanting more of a good thing.

The biggest contradiction to this thought was one particular production of *The King and I*. The cast reprised just about every number in the show. At times the audience joined in for a community sing. Despite the fact that the

The Sound of Music was directed by James B. Randolph at Southwest Miami High School, Miami, Florida.

show ran till after midnight, an unbelievable number of people stayed until the bitter end. An unforgettable experience, yes, but hardly a proper way to portray the great tenderness and emotion of this great Rodgers and Hammerstein classic. It's doubtful that many groups would allow their production to be turned into such a musical free-for-all. However, the temptation to do an encore can be a strong one. If the number is such that an encore would be likely, there is usually one written in the score. It's a good idea to avoid encores when they do not appear in the score and to skip over written ones when the number is not overwhelmingly received.

OTHER DIRECTION TIPS

A person directing a musical cannot always make corrections as he becomes aware of the need for them. He can't arbitrarily break in on rehearsals or work sessions being held by other members of the production staff. For these and other reasons it is wise to have an easy way of recording brief notes for later consultation. Some directors keep the stage manager by their side for just such a purpose. A more convenient method might be to carry around small note papers or a note pad. It may be a little like tying a string around your finger, but when an idea or problem is written down it isn't forgotten. Having a convenient way captures ideas and solutions that can make the production staff function more harmoniously and effectively.

There is always a tendency to become too close and involved in a musical production—to the point where it is difficult to judge how good or bad it really is. Develop your direction skills by this exercise: Tape-record the show, put it aside for about three months, and then play it back. Just like the audience at the time of the show, the playback listener is "seeing" the production for the first time. There probably will be obvious mistakes previously undetected. Then take into account the uncaptured visual mistakes lost to time—and your group's reputation.

In sizing up his responsibility the director should bear in mind that a musical should be paced faster than a play; that the opening number, the first act finale, and the end of the show are usually the most important parts as far as audience retention is concerned; that the numerous changes from part to part, especially the set changes, are potential pitfalls that can drag the show: the "little things" that make an amateur production an *amateur* production. The little things that could have been overcome, but weren't.

And by the very nature of the directing function, there can be only ONE director, one head and one final seat of absolute judgment. Excuses for two directors, such as splitting up the work to get the job done faster; not hurting anyone's feelings; one person can't be at all the rehearsals; etc., can only mean one thing: The group will be incapable of doing their best job and probably shouldn't even attempt a musical. (One slightly disappointing response to the Musical Comedy Production Questionnaire was that 17 groups entertained the folly of having more than one stage director.)

Although there are many musical productions that incorporate two or more directors, this author has never seen any favorable results. Conflicts in individual directors' methods of instruction and differences in their individual conceptions, ever so slight, show through in the final production and are often confusing to the cast.

A director is many things: creative head, arbitrator, psychologist, psychiatrist, and sometimes, just plain mother. In a musical he must work well with others, communicate his ideas in detail, develop the skills of the production staff, win the confidence of his cast so they accept the changes necessary in building a musical, and connect all the various parts together as tightly and smoothly as possible. He must accept a musical as a new and different challenge and plan accordingly.

The Stage Manager

While the director is the creative head and "chairman of the production board," he has a vital counterpart: the stage manager. Some-times this function is falsely dubbed assistant director, student director, production manager, etc., but the only proper name is stage manager.

The professional stage manager is the boss and represents the director once the show reaches opening night. Not only does he call *all* the cues during the performance, but he hires replacement actors, calls brush-up rehearsals, and cares for the upkeep of all the physical production materials (except musical scores).

In nonprofessional productions, the stage manager's authority is greatly reduced, but the function remains basically the same. The nonpro stage manager and one or two assistants are a must for a smooth musical production with hundreds of cues, entrances and exits, set and lighting changes.

The Functions of a Stage Manager

The director must make the cast aware of the stage manager's authority. The stage manager must not abuse this authority and must fall back on the director should a member of the cast or crew need serious reprimanding.

By means of a rehearsal schedule, the stage manager or one of his assistants should make sure the cast members show up at the appointed rehearsal times set by the director, choreographer, or musical director. He should have the rehearsal space clear and whatever props and setting(s) the director has prescribed.

During the blocking of the scene or musical number the stage manager should make note in his script of each movement at the exact line cue. His script is the "bible" of the director's staging. It is used to fill in anyone who missed the original blocking and to correct the action should the actor move on the wrong line during run-throughs. When all the final blocking has been noted, he establishes warning cues for entrances. This is accomplished by making a box in the upper right hand corner of his script. In these boxes he writes the names of the actors or chorus or dancers that are due on stage five pages later. During the production he makes sure these people are in their positions when their warning cue appears on the script page of the action that is taking place on the stage.

In the final production meetings, the lighting, set change, music, and sound effect cues are set. Each cue is sequentially noted in the stage manager's script. Once noted, each is assigned a number that will be given by the stage manager over his headphones. The cue to dim the house lights is cue number one. The cue for

(Figure 4-1)

WEEKLY REHERSAL SCHEDULE
"BELLS ARE RINGING"

Week of February 6–12

MONDAY	TUESDAY	WEDNESDAY	THURSDAY	FRIDAY	SATURDAY	SUNDAY
7:30	7:30	7:30	7:30	7:00	Off	2:30
Little Theatre	*Little Theatre*	*Little Theatre*	*Room 212*	*Music Room*		*Little Theatre*
Director	Director	Director	Director	Musical		Run through
Choreographer				Director		both acts
Musical	Act II, Scene 4	"I'm Goin'	Act II, Scene 7			
Director	"Salzburg"	Back"		Pianist		Everyone.
			Ella	Ella		
"Drop That	Sue	Ella	Jeff	Jeff		
Name"	Sandor					
				Run through		
"Just in Time"	Song &	9:00	*Dance Studio*	solos and duets		
	Dialogue	"Long Before I	Choreographer			
Entire Cast		Knew You"		*Little Theatre*		
			"Salzburg"	Stage Crew		
Costumes will	7:30	Jeff				
be fitted. Non-	*Gym*		Sue	Get sets in		
involved princi-	Choreographer	7:30	Sandor	workable con-		
pals first, then		*Gym*		dition for Sun-		
other cast mem-	Mu-Cha-Cha	Choreographer	*Music Room*	day run-		
bers as can be			Musical	through.		
during and after	Carol	Mu-Cha-Cha	Director			
rehearsal.	Carl					
		Carol	Ensemble			
		Carl	Review all			
	7:30		numbers.			
	Music Room	Musical				
	Musical	Director	*Little Theatre*			
	Director		Stage Crew			
		Off				
	"I'm Goin'		Move sets to			
	Back"		stage.			
	Ella					
	8:30					
	"Long Before I					
	Knew You"					
	Jeff					

the spotlight on the conductor is two. Take the house lights completely out is three. Curtain lights is four. Lift curtain five. Kill spot six. And so on. Most musicals will have from 200 to 400 cues, every one called by the stage manager.

To help with this task, individual sheets for each production station are made up: one for the lighting technician, one for the sound man, one for the fly gallery crew, one for the spot man, and one for the stage crew. These sheets list only the number of the cues that affect that particular production station. Listed is the cue number and exactly what is to be done.

As each cue is encountered, the proper action is called for by the stage manager, "go 36 spot on Higgins; go 37 and 38 fade stage lighting and revolve set."

The stage manager must also keep order backstage and check out all the equipment before the show. Some directors have other assignments for the stage manager, who in turn has his assistants to help him with his duties.

The stage manager should be on the most important side of the stage and have one of his assistants with a headset on the other. A second assistant could be free to round up tardy actors not present for their warning cue or to perform other needed functions or relieve the stage manager if necessary.

Some directors prefer to be their own stage manager. This is usually unnecessary and tends to drag rehearsals. There is more than enough work for a separate person. It is surprising how capable people respond to this responsibility. It is a big job and excellent training for anyone

5 MINUTE CALL

    POSITION CHECK –
        EVERYONE ON STAGE FOR SCENE ONE
        PIT READY
        FLY GALLERY
        LIGHTS
        SOUND
        WARN CUES ① through ⑪

OPENING
  CUE #
  ① DIM HOUSE LIGHTS TO ⅓
  ② CONDUCTOR'S ENTRANCE
  ③ SPOT ON CONDUCTOR
  ④ FLY GRAND DRAPE
  ⑤ LIGHTS TO FULL ON ORCHESTRA SCRIM
  ⑥ READY ON STAGE
  ⑦ FLY MASK DROP BEHIND SCRIM
  ⑧ FADE UP STAGE LIGHTS TO FULL – SCENE 1
      ON MUSIC CUE
  ⑨ KILL SPOT ON CONDUCTOR
  ⑩ TAKE HOUSE LIGHTS OUT
  ⑪ FLY SCRIM

ACT I – SCENE ONE
  ⑫ WARN CONDUCTOR FOR sight cue pick-up on
      MUSIC #2 "WHY CAN'T THE ENGLISH?"
  ⑬ Slow dim to 50% – ALL LIGHTS EXCEPT DOWN RIGHT
      AREA DURING NUMBER
  ⑭ LIGHTS UP FOLLOWING NUMBER
  ⑮ WARN CONDUCTOR for sight cue pick-up on
      MUSIC #3 "WOULDN'T IT BE LOVERLY"
  ⑯ SPOT ON ELIZA
  ⑰ KILL SPOT FOR DANCE
  ⑱ WARN CONDUCTOR FOR MUSIC #3a ON BLACKOUT
  ⑲ BLACKOUT ALL but SMUDGE POT FIRE
  ⑳ KILL FIRE
  ㉑ FLY OUT "COVENT GARDEN" DROP
  ㉒ BRING IN "TOTTENHAM COURT" DROP

SCENE TWO
  ㉓ REVOLVE TURNTABLES ⅓ to "TOTTENHAM COURT"
  ㉔ STAGE LIGHTS UP FOR SCENE 2
  ㉕ WARN CONDUCTOR for sight cue pick-up on
      MUSIC #4 "WITH A LITTLE BIT of LUCK"
      and SEGUE into #4a
  ㉖ BLACKOUT
  ㉗ FLY OUT "TOTTENHAM COURT" DROP

SCENE THREE
  ㉘ REVOLVE TURNTABLES ⅓ to "HIGGINS STUDY"
  ㉙ STAGE LIGHTS UP FOR SCENE 3

(Figure 4-2a)
STAGE MANAGER'S CUES

STAGE

EVERYONE FOR SCENES 1-3 standby on STAGE
    AT 5 MINUTE CALL

⑥ READY ON STAGE
㉓ REVOLVE TURNTABLES ⅓ to
    "TOTTENHAM COURT"
㉘ REVOLVE TURNTABLES ⅓ to
    "HIGGINS STUDY"

Pit

② CONDUCTOR'S ENTRANCE
    BEGIN OVERTURE
⑫ Sight PICK-UP for #2
⑮ " " " #3
⑱ " " " #3a
㉕ " " " #4 and 4a

FLY GALLERY

④ FLY GRAND DRAPE
⑦ FLY MASK DROP
⑪ FLY SCRIM
㉑ FLY OUT "COVENT GARDEN" DROP
㉒ BRING IN "TOTTENHAM COURT" DROP
㉗ FLY OUT "TOTTENHAM COURT" DROP

LIGHTS

① DIM HOUSE LIGHTS to ⅓
③ SPOT ON CONDUCTOR
⑤ LIGHTS FULL ON SCRIM
⑧ FADE UP STAGE LIGHTS TO FULL
    SCENE 1 ON MUSIC CUE
⑨ KILL SPOT ON CONDUCTOR
⑩ HOUSE LIGHTS OUT
⑬ DIM ALL BANKS EXCEPT #8-12 to 50%
⑭ RETURN ALL 50% BANKS to FULL
⑯ SPOT ON ELIZA
⑰ KILL SPOT
⑲ BLACKOUT EXCEPT dimmer #20
⑳ #20 – FAST DIM OUT
㉔ STAGE LIGHTS UP for SCENE 2
㉖ BLACKOUT
㉙ STAGE LIGHTS UP for SCENE 3

(Figure 4-2b)
PRODUCTION CREW CUE SHEETS

who likes a challenge: a must for someone who hopes to direct musicals himself someday.

CASTING

Gathering the cast for a musical presents a few special problems, but the method of selection remains much the same as a play. However, just as the knowledge of the whole field of musical comedy is necessary for the best selection of the musical to present, an extensive knowledge of the show being presented is necessary to choose the best personnel for its production.

From the preproduction meetings, certain character requirements have been established and must be kept in mind. And although the director is to have final say, the judgment of the choreographer and musical director, who must also work with the director's choice, should be considered. The sing and dance choruses should be based on their choices with the director's approval.

THE MECHANICS OF CASTING

Musicals require more people than do straight plays. Would-be performers who wouldn't normally show up for a play are aware of this fact and usually turn out for tryouts in droves. An organized means of processing these people will save everyone's nerves.

Upon arrival at the specified time each person trying out should be given three 3 x 5 cards and a set of duplicated instructions informing him of the casting policies of the group and instructions to fill out the three cards, one each for the stage director, musical director, and choreographer. One side is usually for the prospective cast member's name, address, telephone number, etc. and the other side for any experience or talent he might have.

Soon after the first arrivals have finished filling out their cards the tryouts should begin. If there are people in the group the director knows to be talented (or just willing to give their all) it is good to start with them first. It gets the ball rolling on the right track.

The three cards are distributed to each production staff member. As the named individual tries out, each notes his opinion. A good method is to have the prospects sing and read

individually and then try out for dancing in a group. The people displaying the best movement, as described in the chapter on choreography, can then display their dancing talent separately, if desired.

Elimination of the obvious misfits should be made immediately. A reserve of the best people should be called back for another evening of the same. The ideal system is to allow a full week for casting: Monday, Tuesday, and Wednesday for weeding out the misfits and classifying the possibilities; Thursday and possibly Friday for making the final decision.

HOW BIG A CAST?

For many reasons, sometimes very obscure, people of all ages have an inner drive to participate in a theatrical production. With the recent large increases in professional summer theatres, technical advances of nonprofessional groups, and increasing numbers of high-school productions, interest is at an all-time high. Participation and attendance is rising year by year with no end in sight.

With the increase, however, fewer people want to play Hamlet and more attention has turned to Curly, Billy, Professor Higgins, and Conrad Birdie. The biggest problem is that not everyone can get a part, although some directors try very hard to get everyone in the cast who wants in.

In the musical *Milk and Honey* a herd of sheep is written into the first scene. To this author's knowledge, it is the only musical that calls for a herd of *anything* on stage. The crowd belongs in the audience, not in front of the footlights. Putting them there is a good way to have the cast soon outnumber people in the audience who aren't related to someone on stage. If the group's intention is just to provide a few laughs for the relation, there are much cheaper ways of doing it.

Competition for the best parts is a healthy climate for any group. No director should be required to use everyone who tries out. Missing out on a part one year will motivate an individual to greater achievement and effort in trying out for the next production, even if it's with another group.

The director's duty is to cast the show with the people best suited for the parts as he sees

Stage manager's cues as they would be marked for the first few scenes on the production script for My Fair Lady *(a). And (b) these same cues as they would appear on the individual production crew cue sheets. Numbering each cue keeps everyone alert as to when their numbers are coming up and helps ensure that everything will happen in proper sequence.*

them. The number of the chorus should be set in advance and only the set number should be cast. The chorus may include more people than in the Broadway production where the number of paid actors is kept to a minimum, but the total number should never turn into a herd. The exact number depends on the size of the stage. The larger the stage, the more people in the chorus. On the average stage (35′ proscenium opening), twelve singers and ten to sixteen dancers are plenty.

There are two common practices employed in nonprofessional musical casting that should be abolished: a separate chorus for each number and double leads.

These practices stemmed from trying to give everyone a chance. Both deprive the better people of their personal achievement and weaken the production. People in the chorus should be allowed to do the whole job. It makes their trips to rehearsals worthwhile, and

the best people can be concentrated in one group. Then nobody "wishes they were in a better number," and the costume department is forever grateful.

No one should ever be required to share a lead role. For one person to play the lead on Tuesday, Thursday, and Saturday, whereas another person performs on Wednesday and Friday is one of the most ridiculous ideas any mother has ever pushed through. When this is the case each member of the cast has the tendency to like one lead better than the other; rehearsals are maddening; and duplication of effort slows the progress of the group, sometimes seriously jeopardizing the production.

In double casting someone is always better and they deserve sole possession of the role. Second-bests deserve to be understudies. A good backup crew provides insurance against illness, and it is the accepted practice for the less talented to become better. There is no law

A special casting problem, such as the children in the production of The Music Man, *Lloyd K. Lewis, director, produced at North High School, Springfield, Ohio, may be solved by enlisting the students' young brothers and sisters. The all-boy or all-girl school has another problem. The above production of* Guys *and* Dolls *at all-boy Chaminade High School, Dayton, Ohio, was helped immeasurably by the girls from Julienne High School. Norma Sharkey directed.*

(Figure 4-3)—(Sample instruction sheet)

CASTING POLICY

Our group prides itself on fine musical productions. In order to achieve this goal, full cooperation is required of *every* cast member no matter how large or small the part he or she is assigned.

All casting is based on the judgment of the production staff. No tryouts for specific parts are held. If cast in this show you may be asked to do a principal role, sing or dance in a chorus, or do a walk-on part. If you are not prepared to accept these conditions, please do not waste the time of the production staff and jeopardize yourself for future consideration in other shows.

Each person will be asked to sing and read individually. You may sing a number you have prepared or a number from the show's choral book. Dance tryouts will be held in groups. Close attention will be required to the choreographer at this time. If there is any physical reason you should not take part in strenuous dancing please mark your card "No Dance Tryout."

Fill out the attached 3 x 5 cards as follows:

On the Front Side of Card
  Name
  Address
  Phone Number
  Any evening or Sunday afternoon commitments between now and the
  final performance of this show.

On the Back Side of Card

List any prior dramatic, musical, or dancing experience; then list any other talents or experiences you feel might help the production staff better judge your desire or capabilities.

that says the understudy can't be in the show. Being a member of the chorus and understudy is a lot better than just being a member of the chorus and a lot less depressing than just standing in the wings.

PICKING THE PRINCIPAL CHARACTERS

In a musical, the principal characters are required to perform a variety of tasks. The tasks vary from role to role and from show to show. One director's concept of a given lead character might be different from the concept of another. That's show biz.

Obviously the person who plays a robust Billy Bigelow in *Carousel* would make a poor Riff in *West Side Story*. Billy is a strong singer who doesn't dance and Riff is a strong dancer who doesn't do much singing. Casting these parts is rather clear-cut, but for the most part it is not that easy. Then you have the problem of casting such shows as *I Do! I Do!,* or the

leads in *Annie Get Your Gun, Gypsy, Kismet, Mame, Hello, Dolly!,* or *The Unsinkable Molly Brown*. These characters make the show. Without a strong actor to master the ropes, there wouldn't be enough substance left to provide a dull intermission.

Therefore it is necessary to know in advance the talent required for each principal part. If the requirements can't be filled by the prospects trying out, there are two alternatives: go outside the group to cast the part, or switch to another show. Whatever the choice, it is important to make it during casting rather than leaving the problem to chance or hoping things will work out later.

It is recommended to have a policy whereby no person is trying out for a specific part. It should be made clear that any person trying out may get a lead role or end up in the chorus. Anyone not wishing to try out under these conditions should not waste the director's time.

This way the director has a free hand in casting and can save hard feelings later.

It is unfortunate more people can't be great singers, dancers, and actors rolled into one, but as it stands, such people are rare. (It is also unfortunate that all the people who *think* they possess all these talents aren't rarer.) So the director must decide what talent is most important to each role and cast accordingly from the available talent.

High schools and other youth groups can often improve their musical and have a lot of fun casting teachers, principals, or other school or group personalities in adult roles. For example, it surely doesn't hurt to have a favorite history teacher playing the cop in *West Side Story*. It makes the casting more believable and good box office and publicity, too.

Many Broadway cast albums are full of people who can't sing. However, audiences of nonprofessional musical productions seem to prefer good choral work and a strong baritone voice. To attempt a musical without several good voices is really defeating the purpose of the score.

SPECIAL CASTING PROBLEMS

Many musicals call for the use of children. This problem isn't as big as it might seem. If cast members don't have the needed children in their own families, a simple distress signal in the form of a press release to the local newspaper will usually bring a flock of mothers volunteering the services of their "talented"

offspring. After all, how did Jackie Coogan and Shirley Temple get their start?

In the case of all-boy and all-girl high schools, combined productions have been very successful. In some cases both schools will do a musical production, borrowing the necessary personnel of the opposite sex on a reciprocal basis.

Happy Hunting requires the use of a trained horse. *Gypsy* is almost a zoo set to music. From time to time birds, dogs, monkeys, goats, sheep, and a host of other animals have had their starring moments on the musical stage. Never discount their possible use. Such animals are available in pet stores, zoos, biology departments, amusement parks, stables, animal shelters, and among the friends of the cast. They always lend charm and a bit of professionalism when they are worked into a production. Their owners are usually happy to lend them out for a mention in the program. Bears, apes, and trained horses can still be cast from human(s) plus costume.

LIKE THE ARMY

Everyone can't be cast. The number of cast members must be held within reasonable limits. It is said it takes a battalion of men to keep one soldier supplied on the front lines. Similar is the story of the musical cast and production crew. Every job is important. When each job is put in its proper perspective there will be plenty for everyone to do.

Hill Country Arts Foundation production of Brigadoon *directed by William Y. Hardy at Ingram, Texas.*

CHAPTER V Choreographer

*"Look Ma! I'm Doing
    Choreography"*

Back in 1866 a young theatre manager and a Wall Street broker hired a French ballet troupe to present *La Biche aux Bois,* a popular romantic ballet, at New York's Academy of Music. During the long ocean crossing, the Academy of Music burned down. The producers had an expensive ballet company to pay and no theatre in which to present it.

To solve their problem they persuaded the manager-producer of Niblo's Garden, a highly fashionable theatre of the time, to merge the company into a melodrama he was about to present. The result was *The Black Crook,* the first successful musical entertainment and generally considered the first link in the development of musical theatre as we know it today.

A similar development was unveiled in 1943 when Agnes de Mille's integrated choreography for *Oklahoma!* played such an important part in completing the modern musical theatre concept.

In just about every musical available for production, dance is called upon to provide an extra dramatic dimension. Projecting that dimension, however, is the task nonprofessional groups find the most difficult in staging musicals.

It remains a problem because not many people have been specifically trained in the field, and the mechanics of the problem have appeared sufficiently baffling to scare away all but the most experienced dancers. The root of the problem is simply a fear of something out of the ordinary.

Singing is easily attained from church and school activities and most people will make a wholehearted attempt to sing. Formal high-school and university musical education programs, along with private music teachers, are turning out well-qualified musicians. Acting has had the benefit of organized drama for years, and modern speech and drama departments have never enjoyed stronger backing than they do today.

Choreography, on the other hand, is dif-ficult because it is foreign. It remains foreign, to a large degree, because people don't even try fully to understand its function.

A lot of the confusion stems from the fact that stage dancing is not as socially predominant as some sports or other forms of recreation. Thus vast resources of natural dancing ability go unnoticed and undeveloped. American people, for example, don't normally break into dance or choreographed movements like characters in a musical comedy. In other countries of the world, France, Greece, and Ireland, for example, people are far less inhibited. In some of the unspoiled cultures of Africa, the art of dancing is as basic as the means of communication.

It's a shame dancing isn't more generally accepted because it is an extremely satisfying way to let out energy and emotion. It's fun to do and a type of fun that should be conveyed to the audience.

Most inexperienced nonprofessionals don't visualize themselves with any natural dancing talent, just as most children don't visualize their natural ability to ride a two-wheel bike. Yet just about anybody who can ride a bike well can dance well. It just takes a little perseverance to catch on. The real problem is to get people to realize their ability and put their will to work learning.

Some girls' physical education programs now offer modern dance as part of their curriculum. However, private dancing schools still supply the largest output of broadly trained dancers. Although many talented people have come from these ranks, it is unfortunate that only people wishing to cultivate their dancing ability, and who have the money available to do so, emerge as polished dancers. This represents only a small fraction of the people with natural dancing talent. It is hoped this chapter will help nonprofessional groups cash in on this suppressed natural talent and channel it into better dance numbers, a desperately needed improvement for most groups.

A story of young lovers serves as the basis for the "Marian the Librarian" dance sequence in The Music Man, *as produced by Robbinsdale Senior High School, Robbinsdale, Minnesota. Neal Luebke directed.*

What Is Choreography?

The word choreography is built from the Greek word *choreia* meaning dance. One of its original uses was to describe the direction or arrangement of dances, particularly ballet. However, when applied to modern musical theatre it means much more, i.e., all movement set to music or rhythm. Many times it isn't even "dancing" at all.

The most important point to understand is that choreography is *acting* in the medium of dance, *not* merely unrelated dance interludes in the acting. Ideally, all the musical and rhythmic parts (not just the dances) are choreographed.

Choreographed sequences are usually meant to pick up the pace of the show. They are often called upon to bring the audience more emotionally and physically into the atmosphere or chain of events. Whereas a play can pick up anywhere, a musical usually starts with a big choreographed number designed to set the time, place, and a big chunk of plot. Furthermore, it's a chance to establish a character type

or production mood by what people *do* rather than just what they say, a chance to use exaggeration or fantasy; to convey meaning more effectively; to display a character's exuberance; to utilize extensions of emotion and movement of all types.

The choreographic requirement varies from show to show. There are *dancing shows* such as *West Side Story, On the Town, Sweet Charity,* and others, in which choreography is a prime motivation for selection. Such shows as *The Music Man, Oklahoma!,* and *Damn Yankees* depend heavily on good choreography, but to a lesser degree. Choreography is almost incidental in *My Fair Lady* and about nonexistent in *Riverwind.* So a group can choose as much or as little as they think they can handle. And although choreography will remain a problem until more people become interested enough to develop themselves as choreographers, the problem isn't as big as it may seem. As in learning any uninvestigated field, you are always surprised to discover how much about it you already know.

THE CHOREOGRAPHING TEAM

The main member of the team is the choreographer. He or she is normally responsible for staging all the dances and musical numbers. The director may wish to stage some of the songs, especially if they involve only one or two people, but the bulk of the load should be carried by the choreographer. This practice makes for livelier musical numbers and relieves the director to concentrate his skills on the area in which he is most familiar. It is the accepted professional practice and has certain merits, but, of course, this decision is still that of the director.

Any show with more than three major dance sequences or a large group of dancers should incorporate the services of an assistant choreographer. This second member of the choreographing team should be able to supply additional creative services within guidelines set by the choreographer. Sometimes the two work together to create dances and share the responsibility of setting and teaching the various numbers. Another method is to have the assistant drill the dancers in the numbers already set by the choreographer while the latter creates other musical numbers. The assistant also stands in for the choreographer when he cannot be present for a rehearsal.

Often an assistant choreographer is chosen for his knowledge of a specific type of dance needed in the production and perhaps not included in the choreographer's repertoire. There are times when two assistants are required (or maybe just desired) to provide the necessary creative and training services.

The third member of the choreographing team is the rehearsal pianist, preferably one with a comprehensive knowledge of the mechanics of music. The rehearsal pianist can help the choreographer work out counts, break the whole number down into individual rehearsal passages, or manipulate the score to achieve the desired accompaniment. In rehearsals, he is the choreographer's right arm in varying the tempo to speed the learning process.

A good number of America's leading musical comedy composers started as rehearsal pianists. They probably didn't write their shows to ensure steady work for pianists of today, but there is certainly no better experience in the practical application of music.

The united choreographic effort must strive to elevate the musical numbers and dances to the greatest heights possible. The ability to achieve this goal successfully rests chiefly in three main factors: 1) the talent of the available personnel; 2) the choreographer's ability to adjust to the group; 3) the method of teaching nonprofessionals.

It is always nice to have an abundance of specially trained male and female dancers. As was brought out earlier in this chapter, however, most nonprofessional groups (if any) do not possess such capabilities. Therefore more emphasis necessarily falls on the remaining two factors.

The choreographer must learn about his group and adjust to their talents. He must not set his numbers beyond the group's apparent skill or potential achievement. This theory is in direct conflict with the teaching of the old dance masters, but there usually isn't enough time to build well-rounded dancers; *nor are they absolutely required.*

The sing and/or dance chorus making up many Broadway and most professional summer stock companies are only of high-school or college age. They have more training than nonprofessionals, but this is the broad training required for their chosen career. Specific training for a particular musical doesn't require extensive dance education. It requires a teacher who can bring off the most professional movement possible while maintaining the mood, spirit, and style of the show's musical and dance numbers.

Regarding the mood, spirit, and style, look to the story-line theme, the production guidelines set down in the preproduction meetings, and the music scored for the number. A dance number may be great in itself and completely out of place in a given musical. This violation often occurs when dancing school teachers fill in as choreographers. To them, the dance is the thing. Too often, they don't even read the script through; rather, just the sections that explain the dance. When just the dance explanations are read there is more of a tendency to make slight changes to fit their own steps or style. When mistakes become apparent it's too late to make corrections. The choreographer's concept must be correct from the start.

PREPARING TO CHOREOGRAPH

Unlike the lines of the script or the musical notes of the score, there is very little for the choreographer to go on. Sometimes the complete direction for an important sequence is simply described "dance." It hardly seems fair, but no simple practical way has yet been discovered to pass along this type of information. Perhaps in time performing unions will permit film or videotape to be used for this purpose, but for the time being each choreographer is on his own. And though the job is a bit more difficult, the choreographer's duty to the production demands that he learn as much about the production as possible to ensure that his concepts are correct. This requires a certain amount of research.

There are many ways—both musically and visually—to research the choreographer's ideas to make sure they are on the right track. Usually this research begins with a thorough examination of the piano/conductor score to determine *all* the dance sequences and musical numbers to be staged. This is the basic information required for choreography and the point at which a large number of nonprofessional choreographers doom themselves before they ever get a good start. Perhaps this can best be served by an illustration. It's the first joint rehearsal with the orchestra. The dance numbers are all worked out and highly polished. The orchestra sounds great. Enthusiasm is bursting in the dancers' hearts. There's the cue, and the runthrough is on. "That first 64 bars really looks great. Whoops, what happened to the beat? Where did those trumpets come from? Great day in the morning! Listen to that wild orches-

tration—and look what we're doing onstage. It doesn't match!"

There you have it, the cardinal sin of choreography; working out a number to fit the counts, but not to match the orchestration. The explanation is simple. Whereas the piano part has all the beats, the color of the orchestration (described in detail in the chapter on musical direction) is quick to take command as a number builds. The beats for a light piccolo, stick rhythm, and blaring trumpets and drums can be the same; however, the first suggests small intimate steps whereas the latter demands bold steps and/or big flashy stage crosses. Oh, how many times have you heard the orchestra going wild while the dancers do a few simple turns? The simple solution is to research the orchestration from the conductor's score.

Cast albums also are often a primary source of research, but unfortunately most dance music is not included. If dance music is included, be certain it matches the score. Dance music on many original-cast albums and just about every movie soundtrack album has been altered.

A scene from Oklahoma!, *directed by Julien R. Hughes at Leuzinger High School, Lawndale, California. The overall patterns formed by dancers are more important than individual steps. Better choreography is achieved with several interesting patterns and movements, using simple steps, than when difficult steps are done in place.*

JAMES R. WEBER

Never set dances to commercially recorded scores unless you plan to trim down the production score accordingly.

Other books, programs, publications, etc., with pictures of dance numbers as they appeared in the original production, or pictures of dances as they were performed in the particular period of the show, are also helpful.

Here it might be well to mention that, in just about every case, the dance music in the score was written or arranged to the original choreography. For the Broadway version the choreographer creates with the rehearsal pianist in working up his numbers. The choreographer wants to tell a story in the dance steps he has created from his image of the overall effect. The rehearsal pianist and/or the arranger then composes music that will match, usually building the number from themes and variations in the score. The musical *feelings* painted by the dance music often provide important clues to the present choreographer on which he can begin to base his own impressions and ideas.

It is difficult to visualize how choreography will look on stage. Thus far, human ingenuity has failed to produce little more than crude notes for writing and preplanning. Some people use model stages and small figures. Others name their steps, assign count values, and draw a series of placement and direction-of-movement diagrams. But it still remains a major obstacle to effective musical production. Like any obstacle, the more successfully a choreographer gets around it, the better the finished product. The clearer the choreographer's visualization of his numbers, the easier it is to plan, to communicate with the director, and to teach the cast members. Too many choreographers overlook this vital phase of their preparation duties and arrive at the first rehearsals *knowing that they will be able to work things out*. No professional choreographer would ever attempt such a foolhardy stunt. Let the nonprofessional take heed and grab a note pad.

If it is felt absolutely necessary to have the score recorded for choreographing purposes, have a capable pianist, perhaps the musical director, tape-record all the appropriate dance music. Listening to the tape while following the score often gives insight as to what the composer and original choreographer had in mind. However, the best tools for planning choreography in advance are mathematical counts based on the conductor/piano score. (Actual written cues to movement appear in many scores.)

In general, plan the patterns and overall movement first; not the foot manipulations. Just as in a half-time band show on a football field, musical numbers and dances must be conceived with the total effect rather than individual foot movement in mind. Once the total pattern and reason for the number are determined, the individual steps come easier and new steps often result. When a number is thought of only as a series of steps it automatically restricts itself to known material and is more likely to be tired and boring.

For example, in *West Side Story* you want to portray the emotions of two street gangs. The procedure is not to see if you can toughen up classic ballet steps, but to imagine how two street gangs would act, and then convert that action to dance. The same is true for *Bye Bye Birdie*. You don't just take the dance hall rock-and-roll and put it on stage. You *adapt* the steps according to the techniques of choreography. This is done by imagining what the overall effect of a number should be and then creating action and steps that fit. Conversely, if you just try to think of known steps, the excitement of invention will be lost, both to you and your audience.

Once the overall movement and the *story* of the number are sketched out, work up a series of steps or movements that fit the music, ranging from easy to difficult. These will be used in tryouts and the first rehearsal sessions to determine the learning capacity of the group. It is most important to be specific and to know what is to be done so instruction can be given with confidence. When cast members sense this air of confidence they will work harder to elevate themselves to what is being taught. If rehearsal sessions are unorganized and a variety of steps is tried before anything definite is set, the individuals' output is likely to drop below their natural talents. Always have each rehearsal planned in advance. Always have enough new material to make each teaching rehearsal worthwhile.

Another point to consider in preplanning is what to do about topical dance sequences. Musical comedies that trade on socially "in" dance practices or fads often build production numbers around dance trends of the times—which may have since become obscure. These are difficult numbers to get across in revival productions. Whether it be an authentic cakewalk, waltz, tango, twist, or frug, there is a problem in finding the right steps, and if you do, the audience often has a problem fitting the number into their present-day thinking. Certainly the meaning is not projected as universally as when the particular fad was current.

When a musical is not a period piece and incorporates these obscure fad sequences, some consideration should be given to updating the number (and music) to something more modern. Such numbers are usually found in loosely constructed shows. Updating can often convert a liability into an asset.

Likewise, other cuts and alterations are always in the picture if they can be used to the betterment of the whole production. When the choreographer and director do their homework and plan ahead, these opportunities will become apparent, and, once again, the production will be better for it.

CASTING DANCERS

Since dancers do not usually exist in sufficient quantities, everyone should be required to try out for dancing. This can be done in groups and with some nonrelated steps at first. However, final selection should be based on some of the steps planned for the show. The basic Charleston is a good series to test movement. It can be taught quickly to a group and tests ability to shift weight, move, and keep pace in a variety of tempos.

When casting dancers, judge the nonexperienced person's ability to move. Physical limitation such as stiffness of motion, extreme pigeon toes, walking on the heels, inability to shift weight easily, and obviously poor reflexes should determine the first to be eliminated. Overweight people are usually light on their feet and make good dancers, but should also be eliminated unless specifically called for in the script or to meet the director's concept for a certain dancing part.

Some qualities to look for when casting dancers are: ability to shift weight, agility,

Scene from Guys and Dolls, *directed by Robert R. Buseick at Beaverton High School, Beaverton, Oregon. Risqué numbers involving a striptease flavor can usually be handled tastefully. Most numbers calling for this sort of specialty can also be done as a vamp, or otherwise altered to meet a local situation.*

JAMES R. WEBER

The stylized movement of "The Small House of Uncle Thomas," from The King and I, *produced by Leuzinger High School, Lawndale, California, and directed by Julien R. Hughes.*

good reflexes, balance, good rhythm, and the ability to learn quickly. Desire can also mean a great deal and can overcome just about all but the most restrictive physical limitations. Look for strong desire and cultivate it. Sometimes even graduates of dancing school, without desire, should be bypassed for a likely prospect willing to give his all.

SOME THOUGHTS BEFORE REHEARSALS BEGIN

Whereas it is the overall job of the director to move or pace the show, a great deal of the job falls into the hands (and feet) of the choreographer and his assistants, especially in shows in which the dance numbers are up tempo (faster pace). The director's job in moving the show is to eliminate waste between numbers (or parts), whereas the choreographer must move the show within the numbers.

The choreographer moves each individual number by pacing the amount and size of the movement, excitement, and interesting action. Nonprofessional choreographers seem to oper-

ate between two extremes. On the one hand, a singer may come center stage to render his tender ballad with only a minimum of body gestures; on the other, the singer will run all over the stage apparently looking for a clear exit. Both are done. The general rule is to use the number for what it's *worth within the direction style.* If the show is stylized, the musical numbers must keep within the style. Otherwise, movement should occur each time the music or lyrics suggest that a movement is in order. Characteristics in the music inspire dance. Lyrics suggest the movement within a song.

Dances move the show by their vitality and patterns. A tap dancer merely beating out taps doesn't mean much, but the same beats tied in with telling a story, characterizing some action, or using props and/or the set create interest and help move the number. Perhaps the oldest means to this end is to make an easy task look difficult by doing a "difficult" step until the audience applauds. A more modern means is to use exciting dance patterns, perhaps with a number of contrasting things happening at once, to dazzle the audience, to have more action on stage than the human eye can encompass at once.

If the eye is permitted to focus on a central person, the remaining group on stage performs a more moderate movement. If the group is performing movement in unison, there must be sufficient new and different movement to keep the viewer interested. Intricate movement of feet may be an achievement, but it is *the overall movement and the movement pattern* that makes an exciting dance or musical number. There is a general tendency for nonprofessional choreographers to concentrate too much on teaching steps and not move their dancers around enough.

The singing chorus in a scene (and the dancing chorus the while filling the background) must work with the number, not merely stand there. They can move in formation, clap their hands, stamp their feet, parade on and off, or even sway side to side in the old-fashioned way.

The lilt of movement can sparkle what otherwise would be a dull number. If it is deemed better not to have a chorus participating in the number, it would probably be better to remove them from the stage.

Whenever the chorus enters or exits a scene in progress they should drift on a few at a time, never all at once unless the script calls for them to rush on. Never have a chorus come on in lines or globs. Elephants in a circus come in trunk and tail. Actors in musicals enter with meaning and direction.

When the nonprofessional gets the dance music of the original production he can either match the concept of the original production or adjust the music to fit his own concept. Adding or deleting repeats, deleting sections, inserting breaks in the music, adding special orchestral sound effects, or a host of other changes (that the musical director can easily pass on to his orchestra) can be used to tailor the score and choreography to the skills of any group.

The stage is no football field (even though dancers often work a lot harder than football players). Many dance movements are potentially dangerous when attempted by the unskilled. Spectacular effects make a better show,

but certain types of lifts, catches, splits, body impact, tumbling, sharp props (such as knives, swords, etc.), and others could be the cause of serious accident, one that would eliminate a valuable cast member or even cause a lifelong injury. Discipline and detailed teaching are a must.

SOME BASIC PRINCIPLES OF CHOREOGRAPHY

Up until now the discussion has centered on what should be considered and take place before the first rehearsal. The research and planning put the choreographer on top of his job, but nothing is quite the same as developing the various numbers with live dancers— the human factor. Here is found the heart and joy, the madness, the exasperation, the challenge, the fun of being a choreographer.

The best thing is to get acquainted quickly and go right to work as described in the *Teaching Method* section of this chapter. During a break about midway into the session, spend about fifteen to twenty minutes explaining the dances and musical numbers. Answer questions and make sure you convey the idea that you are always open to suggestion. Some of the cast may have had dance instructions, others often discover their natural ability to communicate by means of dance movements. If suggested movements don't fit, perhaps they will lead to something that does. Likewise, a step or series of steps that the choreographer has preplanned might be altered as a result of inspiration at the time of rehearsal.

Of course, every musical number and dance is different, and no single number can incorporate all the techniques of choreography, but a standard approach to staging might involve one of the following possibilities: the opening lead-in or buildup, creating a *story line,* platooning couples or groups, dancing in unison, challenge, patterns, slow motion, solo or specialties, tableau or stop action, parade or chase, using the set, production numbers, stylized movement, or your own method of invention. Let's look at each a little closer.

The Opening Lead-in or Buildup. Few numbers, if any, maintain the same force all the way through. They usually start modestly and build to a climax. Sometimes the first 32

Scenes from the production of How to Succeed in Business Without Really Trying, *directed by Jack Nakano for Youth Theatre Productions, Santa Barbara, California. Virtually every move of such a rapid-fire-paced show is choreographed. Every actor must play the scene hard on each cue—requiring special direction or choreography for each person onstage.*

bars or so are not actually dancing at all, but a dramatic sequence that eventually breaks into dance, people getting into position, or one person starting the action with the others gradually joining in. Quite often the first 32 to 64 bars are simple steps executed in a relatively small area and, as the orchestration builds, some stage crosses, broader traveling steps, and perhaps some lifts and big turns are added, gradually working into some other techniques.

Creating a Story Line. This technique is the stock-in-trade of a ballet choreographer. Musicals that have true ballets, such as *Carousel, Half-a-Sixpence, Golden Boy, On the Town, Flower Drum Song,* and others, rely on story continuity. The same general result can be obtained with other dance styles such as the silent movie sequence in *Goldilocks,* the opening to *Guys and Dolls,* or the dancing part of Susan in *Finian's Rainbow* in which musical action replaces lines of a script. The technique may just show what goes on at a barn dance, as in "The Farmer and Cowman" in *Oklahoma!* or the events of a company picnic as in "Once-a-Year Day" from *Pajama Game.*

When story-line choreography is called for in the script there is usually a rather complete description, sometimes worked in with dialogue. However, the choreographer is free to establish a story line (that fits the show's construction) to help him work out any number. Such a story line provides method and a point of reference to more creative choreography.

Platooning Couples or Groups. This technique is used in virtually all major dance sequences. It is implemented by breaking down the dance chorus into a number of smaller groups (perhaps incorporating some of the more agile sing chorus members) which perform in turn for part of the number. Not only does this allow everyone to get a good breath before a smash finish, but it gives the choreographer flexibility in his staging and the opportunity to use the special talents of more accomplished personnel. The most obvious example that comes to mind is the "Tradition" number from *Fiddler on the Roof.* No one really displays any specific talent in this one, but the mamas, the papas, the sons, and the daughters are platooned beautifully.

Dancing in Unison. The best example of dancing in unison is the kick line such as used in *Fiorello!* and school marching groups. It is also quite impressive in folk dancing as in the Jewish *Milk and Honey* or the Greek *Illya Darling.* But one of the most outstanding uses of this technique was the finale to the "Grand Imperial Cirque de Paris" number in *Carnival.* The technique was built into gradually with a wheel pattern of three people at center and all the other cast members joining on two at a time rather like the chorus girl skaters in an ice show. Then the impressive line, arm in arm, did a short series of steps that brought them front stage where they did several scissor kicks climaxed by the collapse of the whole line flat on their backs (safely and with grace) like a picket fence snapped from its anchor. They sat up once more to the flutter of reeds and piccolos and fell back exhausted at the final blasting chord. Of course the number was a show-stopper every time. And its success was largely due to the power of the dance-in-unison ending. Many people feel that dance in unison is difficult to accomplish. It does take a certain amount of practice, but getting the group arranged according to size—taller in the middle ranging to short on both ends—is the major hurdle. Dancers also seem to learn this technique faster, too, because if they don't they're likely to get stepped on.

The Challenge. The best example of the challenge is "The Dance at the Gym" from *West Side Story* where two platoons of dancers countercross each other and otherwise try to outdo each other in dance. It's an "anything-you-can-do-I-can-do-better" situation with the power of two opposite forces superimposing each other. It is also frequently used with small groups of dancers or perhaps just two leaping past each other in the air. It's a beautiful method for displaying conflict between two characterizations. However, it's a technique that can easily be tiresome, so be careful of overuse.

Patterns. Forming patterns, such as wheels (either the spokes or the rim), four or five small groups (similar to square dancing), or a weave pattern for couples waltzing is a technique that adds interest to simple steps that would tend to be boring if done in place. Perhaps it could best be described as the choreographer's method of composition. Similar to the artist or the photographer, the choreographer must maintain a stage that is pleasing to look at. By balancing the stage and keeping his dancers moving in and out of various patterns, new interest is constantly being created, keeping the audience involved in the number.

Slow Motion. This technique isn't used very much because there isn't much opportunity. When it is used it certainly is effective for the simple reason that it is rare. Paris' seductive "Lazy Afternoon" number from *The Golden*

Apple and the prizefight number from *Golden Boy* are two of the best examples seen on Broadway. A slow-motion effect obtained by use of strobe lights has also been used in a number of musicals, most famously in *Gypsy* to create passage of time.

Solos or Specialties. There are times when a solo or specialty such as *Kiss Me Kate's* "Too Darn Hot" tap dancer or the "Tango" in *The Boy Friend* are called for in the script. There are also opportunities, similar to the platooning technique previously described, to work a solo or specialty into a major number. A single person with, say, acrobatic tumbling skills can add a bit of the spectacular with just a few stage crosses. Largely this is left to the individual talent available. The strip-teases of "Whatever Lola Wants, Lola Gets" from *Damn Yankees* and "Take Back Your Mink" from *Guys and Dolls* also fall under the specialty area. It's a matter of coming up with the right moves or toning down the drum part to match the choreography that is used instead.

Parade or Chase. The Macy's parade in *Here's Love* and the chase of Harry Beaton in *Brigadoon* constantly add new interest as each succeeding group of dancers enters the stage. The technique seems to add a rare action and pulls the audience into the stage quicker than most others. They must watch closely or they might miss something. When the choreographer makes each sequence exciting, he will be well rewarded by applause and a sense of accomplishment. Here again the technique can't be used in every show lest it become familiar and overdone.

Tableau and Stop Action. The "Ascot Gavotte" from *My Fair Lady* is one of the most engrossing and well-publicized bits of choreography ever staged. Yet hardly anything happens—just a stage full of well-dressed spectators strutting around, freezing in their tracks from time to time. It's simple, it's brilliant, it's the undisputed classic of the technique. However, the method has also been used in *No Strings, Hello, Dolly!, Skyscraper,* and a host of others. The impact of the whole stage freezing on a given note, you might well say, "gets them" every time. Usually it's done two or three times to establish the style. There is also much to be said, however, for the punch of a single dose as in the "Coming Home" number in *The Most Happy Fella.* It is a striking technique, but working out the unison halt with non-pros may turn out to be a sizable task.

Using the Set. The orchestra pit runway and train sequence in *Hello, Dolly!,* the swings over the orchestra pit in *Little Mary Sunshine,* the platforms of *The Roar of the Greasepaint–The Smell of the Crowd,* and the library set in *The Music Man* are all good examples of using the set in the design of choreography. For those who know them (from the TV late shows, of course) the old Fred Astaire movies are another good example. Then, too, the revolving stage of *All American* and sliding stage of *Subways Are for Sleeping* offer interesting treadmill effects. A bit sophisticated for most non-pro groups, but a tremendous technique for those who can work it out.

Stylized Movement. The "March of the Toys" from *Babes in Toyland,* Bob Fosse's "Steam Heat" from *Pajama Game,* and "The Small House of Uncle Thomas" from *The King and I* probably are the three best-known examples of stylized movement; the numbers are built completely on clever style. It is a rare brand of choreography and the product of the masters in the industry. Nonprofessional choreography can do little else than try to reproduce these works as accurately as possible. Also, in shows that satirize other shows, such as *The Boy Friend* and *Little Mary Sunshine,* it is imperative that style be maintained.

Production Numbers. Opinions differ widely on just what constitutes a production number. For some, every big number is a production number, but it is really in a class by itself. By reputation the biggest production numbers, with fantastic costumes, waterfalls, and cast of hundreds, are staged at the *Lido* and *Folies Bergères* in Paris. The Ziegfeld numbers in *Funny Girl,* *Mame*'s "Open a New Window," the coronation scene in *Camelot,* and the wedding in *The Sound of Music* are in the mold of a true production number. Quite often they are comprised of pageantry more than actual dancing. A production number is no place to spare expense. Nothing looks worse than a cheap or skimpy production number. Spectacle is all you've got to go on.

Method of Invention. Michael Kidd's choreography for *Li'l Abner* has to be one of the more inventive jobs ever done. Virtually every step was an extension of normal body movement, all completely built from the style and characterization of the show: a perfect example of what can be done around the simplest of moves. At the other extreme, some of the wilder inventions are the overly athletic "Spanish Panic" in *Once Upon a Mattress* and male dancers in toe shoes used in *Anyone Can Whistle.* The point here is not the boundaries of the specific examples, but a range to trigger the choreographer's own capacity for invention. Too much choreography is dependent on

Quick excitement, fast stage crosses, wide movement, and clever steps are required for a dance specialty such as "Who's Got the Pain (When They Do the Mambo)?" from Damn Yankees. *On the other hand, a song-and-dance number such as "When I'm Not*

Near the Girl I Love, I Love the Girl I'm Near" calls for easy, gentle, graceful moves. *Scene is from* Finian's Rainbow. *Both were directed by Patrick S. Gilvary for the University of Dayton Players, Dayton, Ohio.*

known and proven steps. Perhaps this is because many choreographers have felt that it must be this way. It needn't. There are only two restrictions: 1) the construction and characterization of the show and 2) the limitations of the dancers, plus, of course, the music on the page.

A favorite example of invention is toe tapping. It's obvious that if everyone on stage were merely tapping their toes, not much would be communicated to the audience. To choreograph the move it might need to be exaggerated to a stomp, perhaps with the addition of a hand clap. Broaden the move with a little jazzy or shoulder action. Travel it across the stage by touching the stomp lightly on the floor while sliding on the second foot. Touch the toe. Touch the heel. Touch either side of the foot. Tap in front, tap in back, tap directly down. Add characterization—backwoods awkwardness for *Li'l Abner,* elegance for *Hello, Dolly!,* a little frug for *Bye Bye Birdie.* Platoon the dancers with perhaps a solo or specialty here and there: a challenge, some patterns, and the big finish.

That's the feel of it. Care to start with a hand clap? Good luck!

THE TEACHING METHOD

The choreographer must approach the cast with the same type of basic instruction as the director and, if possible, even more so. Every movement should be demonstrated. No details should be overlooked. The instruction should be slow, deliberate, and reflect complete confidence in the group with the assurance they will eventually achieve the desired results.

The first rehearsal or so can be used to teach harder steps to be practiced individually at home. The group should be advised these are the hardest steps they will be asked to learn and that the rest is all downhill.

In short, work on the more difficult dance steps and musical numbers' movements first. Starting on the most difficult steps first provides more time to achieve the desired results. Insert them into the various numbers as they occur in the rehearsal schedule. As the most difficult is conquered it provides the cast with a feeling of accomplishment and is great for the morale of the show.

These first sessions should be fun rather than discouraging, and no attempt should be made to polish the steps. When the group understands and retains the mechanics of a step, move to the next one. Five or six difficult steps are enough for the first session. At the end of the session, each person should be reviewed individually to make sure the material has been absorbed and correctly understood.

The first few minutes of three or four succeeding rehearsals should be used to check the achievement of these difficult steps. As steps are polished, or dropped, other difficult steps are inserted in this kick-off period. The remaining time should be spent in setting and polishing the particular numbers at hand, supposedly with some of the first difficult steps already incorporated into a series of movements as the number takes shape.

The basic formula in setting the complete number is: teach for understanding, enthuse with desire, push hard for accuracy and polish.

With a definite plan in mind, the actual blocking of musical numbers begins. If the dance or movement is for a song, the job is easy. The lyrics usually suggest movement of some type. Movement cues can be set to a specific word or phrase, whereas in dance numbers everything is usually taught to number counts that the choreographer has preplanned to match the mechanics and personality of the score.

Break the number down into units of 8 (into units of 12 for ¾ time). Block out 24 counts at a time. Make sure everyone understands the mechanics of each 24-count sequence. Encourage questions and single out selected dancers to run through the sequence individually. Have the entire group mark (walk or move slowly) the steps through, as slowly as necessary for understanding. After three or four sequences are set, put them together. Speed up the counting a little and get each section of the dance running smoothly on counts alone.

Now it is time for a good rehearsal pianist. When music has been added, work each section at a slower tempo than the speed achieved by just using counts. As the sections are put together the speed is increased until the normal dance tempo is realized.

The varying of tempo converts the dancers from reliance on counts to reliance on the music. It also helps prevent the action from running away from or falling behind the conductor during the performances.

Quite obviously this doesn't leave much room for the use of a tape recorder. Such a marvelous instrument is a valuable tool for the choreographer's use in preparing his dances or numbers, but it's a machine that cannot adjust to the dancers. The dancers must adjust to the machine all at once. This is much more difficult than adjusting gradually to a patient rehearsal pianist. Even a series of recordings at different tempos is no real substitute for a

Effective acrobatic stunts may be worked into some numbers, as in this scene from South Pacific, *as directed by John S. Girault at Greeley Central High School, Greeley, Colorado.*

person who can provide the correct tempo, whatever it may be. Also, the time spent trying to find the precise cue on the tape is wasted time. There is a time to record and a time to teach dance. In a musical, it is a time to teach dance.

CHOREOGRAPHIC ANATOMY

As was mentioned before, dancing is the rare talent needed for musical comedy production. The tendency is to turn to someone who is labeled a dancer or dancing teacher. Many dancing teachers do not make good choreographers. Once a specific person has been named to the part, it is difficult to make a change. The selection of the person to fill the job should be a considered one.

Places to look, other than dancing schools, include: retired (or willing) professionals; physical education teachers trained in modern dance techniques; experienced students; a nonprofessional dancer who has done the musical with another group or has become skilled over a number of other shows; a person so familiar with the show to be presented that he can guide a young dancing teacher in the correct steps and dance patterns on stage.

The key point to remember is that dances are not separate entities in themselves. They are parts in the musical's construction and should advance the musical's construction within the style and story line of the number. Dance numbers in an integrated musical are not showcases for local dancing schools.

Dancing requires a different use of body muscles. Dancers do well to warm up their muscles for this unaccustomed and more strenuous body movement. It helps if the individuals get into shape before a show goes into rehearsal. But regardless of what physical shape the dancing personnel is in, a warm-up session should precede each dance rehearsal. There are many exercises for warm-up activities, but the best are slow bends or stretches that gradually pick up in speed as the muscles loosen. Five to ten minutes of warm-ups should be encouraged prior to each rehearsal session.

The best way to teach nonprofessionals is to start slowly without music and work up the cast's skill to the desired pace. Cut speed and work the number with a rehearsal pianist.

Build achievement with the music and run through the number about five times at the desired speed. (Three- to five-minute rests between run-throughs are recommended for older members of the dance chorus.) If the choreography fits the group, even the slowest dancers should be performing with some degree of proficiency at this stage. If the prescribed movement is too difficult for several dancers, *stop* and prepare simpler movements for the next rehearsal.

If a complete number is beyond the group's achievable skill, delete the number from the show. If the number is necessary, secondary possibilities are: cut the tempo, drastically shorten the number, or fill the dance time with production gimmicks or actor bits that would fit the show's construction.

AND-A ONE, TWO, THREE . . .

Choreography is too often thought of as something people do with their feet. Hopefully the reader now recognizes it as much more. It is a problem in musical production and will remain so until more people learn enough to try their hand. Schools and little-theatre groups have spent years developing well-qualified directors. It shouldn't take nearly as long to grow a good crop of choreographers —because it's much more fun.

CHAPTER VI Musical Director

"Face the Music and . . ."

There's one thing about a musical: you can't do one unless you have an orchestra—or at least a piano or two. Or to quote the fellow who said "up is up," a musical is not a musical without music.

Some groups reject the idea of doing a musical because they don't know where to get an orchestra. Statistics suggest that it shouldn't be too hard. *The American Music Conference* in their 1967 annual report estimated there were currently 43,900,000 amateur musicians in the United States, compared with 20,000,000 in 1950. They say "an amateur musician is someone who plays a musical instrument six or more times a year (either in private or with organized music groups), or someone who is receiving instrumental instruction." One out of every 4.6 Americans is an amateur musician.

Of course not all these people are skilled enough to play a musical score, but the number of people who can is growing every day.

High schools and colleges seem to have the easiest job of assembling suitable musical orchestras. Little theatre and community theatre groups seem to have the most difficult time in putting together and controlling an orchestra. High schools and colleges have captive musicians. They need not compete with the type of family responsibilities that plague adults who play for most little and community theatre groups.

According to the *American Music Conference,* "one out of every two high schools will have stage orchestras by 1970." In 1967 there were "an estimated 70,000 large music groups, including 51,000 marching and concert bands, 7,500 elementary, junior high and high-school orchestras, and 11,500 stage bands . . . plus thousands of string, percussion, woodwind and brass ensembles."

College groups can draw on more experienced musicians, but they face competition from the vast amount of other campus activities. Also, many capable musicians work their way through college playing dance jobs for pay. These jobs always conflict with prime production dates.

In other groups the problem is largely one of rounding up capable musicians and getting everyone together for rehearsals and performance dates. The organization problem is one that should be settled far in advance. Some idea of where the necessary musicians will come from is a *prerequisite* for selecting the musical to be presented. Perhaps someday little theatre groups, and maybe even some college groups, will be able to call on high-school students to provide the orchestral accompaniment.

If the group needs a musical director, the following sources are worth investigation: 1) music teachers, both regular school system teachers and private instructors; 2) gifted college students; 3) professional musicians; 4) church choral directors; 5) vocal coaches; or 6) a working member of the community with a musical background. These are all sources of prospective musical directors, assistant musical directors, or just the person to fill the missing orchestra chair.

SCOPE OF THE MUSICAL DIRECTOR'S DUTIES

The musical director is responsible for all things musical: the orchestra, the singing chorus, and the whole overall sound of the production. His chief duties break down thus:

1) Determines the size and content of the orchestra.
2) Coordinates the musical score.
3) Coordinates and directs orchestra rehearsals.
4) Represents his musicians and choral staff in the production.
5) Schedules and presides over singing chorus rehearsals.
6) Advises other members of the production staff.
7) Conducts the orchestra during performances.

What Size Orchestra?

The basic decision here is whether to have an orchestra or just a piano accompaniment. The main factor in this decision is not which would be better, but which can be assembled. A well-rounded 30-piece orchestra is ideal (an original Broadway orchestra usually ranges from about 25 to 30 pieces), but limitations such as available personnel, budget, or lack of space often require use of smaller musical groups.

The Musical Comedy Production Questionnaire showed that 105 groups usually used a full-sized orchestra, compared to 17 groups who used a piano or organ plus rhythm section, and 14 groups used one or two pianos only. Instrumentation in the full orchestra varies with the show being presented. When piano and/or organs were used with a rhythm section, the instruments were usually bass, drums, and/or guitar. Sometimes an accordion or harp was also used.

A theatre orchestra is not the same as a concert orchestra. Its purpose is to provide accompaniment and "musical color." In a concert orchestra, for example, more strings are needed to balance additional brass and other wind instruments. In a pit orchestra the piano, drums, violins, cello, and bass provide the basic melody and harmony line, while the other instruments provide "interest." Flutes, clarinets, oboe, etc., playing occasionally, as written in the score, distinguish the sound, while brass and other winds add special effects, more robust sound for big dance numbers, and interludes.

If the ideal 30-piece orchestra is impractical, build the orchestra starting with the basic elements: piano, rhythm, and strings. Substitute woodwinds for strings *only if absolutely necessary.* By studying the instrumentation (better still, the whole score) in advance, the qualified musical director can determine where he can "double up" (one musician playing two or more instruments), if the music can be handled by fewer players, or where additional players will be needed. For example, the score may require that a clarinet player also have a flute and a sax in his part. If the chosen clarinetist doesn't possess the extra talents, one or two extra players—a flute and/or sax player—will be required.

However, as more and more wind instruments are incorporated into the orchestra, additional strings are required to maintain balance. The people on stage need a strong beat. The larger the orchestra of nonprofessional players, the more difficult it is to maintain the beat.

Also, great care should be taken not to make the orchestra so large that it overpowers stage activity.

Some musicals call for the use of rare or difficult musical instruments. Capable musicians who play the harp, oboe, viola, bassoon, some alto and bass saxophones, and even violin are sometimes not to be found within the school or group that wishes to do a score in which these instruments add important color. Before these instruments are eliminated or another instrument substituted, some investigation is in order to fill the orchestration as written.

School music teachers, private music teachers, or the musicians' union might be willing to supply an advanced student, professional musician, or member of the community who would be capable of playing the part. One high-school or college group might trade an oboe player for a couple of violin players, etc. When the proper emphasis is placed on audience acceptance instead of the "we're-going-to-do-this-with-what-we-have-available" attitude, this type of mutual help is not at all out of line, especially when it helps both groups do a better show.

If the group does decide to use a musicians' union "ringer," be sure that all details are understood well in advance. Their time is money, and things are likely to get out of hand timewise if some basic understanding, such as a flat fee, or ceiling charge can't be worked out in advance. Paying a specialist can be worthwhile in some shows. If the situation can be avoided it can save hard feelings from the unpaid musicians and other difficulties that could arise. Usually some nonprofessional will sit in for the fun and experience.

Coordinating the Musical Score

During the reading sessions the musical director must coordinate the orchestration. This is necessary for a number of reasons:

1) Printed piano accompaniment, which is often supplied by the leasing agent, does not always agree with the manuscript conductor's score, which in turn does not exactly agree with some of the orchestral parts. Leasing agents have several copies of this material for each show. Although most are photocopies of the original material, some extra printed and hand copies have been prepared to meet demand. The resulting inconsistency should be weeded out before the musicians really have a chance to learn their parts.

Tom Sawyer, *directed by W. L. Kellogg at Westside High School, Omaha, Nebraska.*

2) Similarly, chorus books do not always agree with the score or with each other.

3) Orchestra parts and the conductor's score have been used many times. They are supposed to be clean, yet you will usually find numerous cuts, repeats, etc., from previous performances.

4) In many scores the bars are not numbered or otherwise noted where a particular part is to come in. In such cases, distinctive cues should be inserted.

If a full orchestra is not being used and the piano is to fill in for missing instruments to complete the melody and beat of the orchestration, a piano/conductor score should be used by the pianist. The regular piano part usually doesn't provide enough detail to allow this type of flexibility.

Professional musicians can play louder and softer than nonprofessional musicians. They play for talented people. They improvise and accent the score with their years of musical training.

Most nonprofessionals have to "play hard" to achieve certain solid tones. They are tied to the pages that unfold before them. When this is the case (in any kind of music, really) some passages become overpowering, either for the people on stage to try to sing over, or for the musicians in the pit, who just can't quite cut it. Solutions are to raise or lower an octave or leave out certain instrument parts as written. Why fight it? A first-class trumpeter can play high pianissimo but the average amateur cannot.

The musical director is also responsible for the physical score music books. These books are expensive to prepare and costly to replace should they be lost or damaged. Musicians should be encouraged to rehearse at central music rooms where tight control can be exercised over these books. After the final performance the musical director should make sure all musical parts are returned to the stage manager or director.

Preparing the Orchestra

The musical director must schedule and preside over all orchestra rehearsals and reading sessions. The total number of hours used to prepare the orchestra varies with the type of group. The Musical Comedy Production Questionnaire indicated that most high schools spend better than 20 hours in reading and proficiency sessions before the orchestra joins the cast in joint rehearsals. Most college groups spend 15 to 18 hours, whereas community groups spend only 8 to 10 hours prior to the first joint orchestra-cast rehearsal. Of course, the rehearsal pianist is not included here; he is brought into rehearsals much earlier.

There is a tendency for musical directors, especially college and community theatre baton whirlers, to put off orchestra rehearsals until the last two weeks or so. The result is an unprepared orchestra that gets better with each performance. This is a sign the orchestra could have used more rehearsal in the beginning. The opening-night audience deserves just as good a job as the closing-night audience.

It's a shame there isn't a better way to give the orchestra more credit for the terrific task they must perform, but that's been the story of pit orchestras for more than a century. Give the audience the best possible performance, even though the people on the stage take all the bows. Often nonprofessional productions could be vastly improved if the orchestra would spend more time in polishing the score and depend a little less on sight reading the difficult handwritten manuscript scores found in virtually every musical.

The real goal is to have the orchestra in a state of readiness on the day they are to join the cast. In order to achieve this end, the orchestra must rehearse enough to be really familiar with the music, not just be able to play it acceptably. That is, solid enough for good support without stopping stage activities and flexible enough to vary tempo and make minor adjustments in the score.

In this regard, high-school musicians are accustomed to practicing their individual parts prior to the first full orchestra rehearsal. To a lesser degree, this is also true of college and community theatre players. Individual advance preparation makes life easier for everyone concerned, especially if mistakes in the score are weeded out first.

The orchestra should then rehearse with the cast for *at least a week to ten days* prior to opening night. The people in the pit may not need it, but the people on stage surely do. In such rehearsals the cast can finally come through. It is in these final rehearsals that they gain real confidence and become capable of turning out a polished performance. These rehearsals can also be a terrible drag and nerve-shattering experience that gives the production's momentum a flat tire. If stage personnel don't know their music, lines, and movements, it's virtually a waste of time for the orchestra to be there. This putting together process is either stimulating, and therefore efficient, or a setback for everyone concerned.

The Musicians' Interest

The musical director must represent the interests of his musical family, both the orchestra and the singers. He must learn the capabilities of each member of both groups and help the director use them to the production's best advantage. Musicians can play too long. Cast members can strain their voices. It is up to the musical director to prevent these abuses from happening. He must also see that the stage director does not place the singers so they cannot follow his direction during vocal numbers.

As was touched on earlier, the musical director may need to do some "weeding" in the orchestrations so his musicians can handle the score. These orchestrations were written for highly skilled professionals and some passages may be completely out of the range of nonprofessionals. Certain parts for some numbers, particularly dance numbers, are almost completely written in the upper register. Many times this is not really necessary, and the music can be lowered an octave or transposed into another key. Such concern on the part of the musical director will save his musicians so they can get through the complete score without running out of steam. It will also make for a better *standard* of performance.

Other Members of the Production Staff

The musical director is the final authority on all things musical, just as the director is the final authority on all other matters in the stage production. The director is still final authority on whether any particular section of music or musical number will be included in the production, but the musical director has the final say on how it is sung and/or played. This is how the production staff is interdependent on each

Here's Love *as staged by Scott McCoy for St. Paul's East Side Theatre, St. Paul, Minnesota.*

The King and I *directed by Julien R. Hughes at Leuzinger High School, Lawndale, California.*

member and why complete harmony and co-operation is so vital.

By the nature of the two functions, the musical director will work with the choreographer more than the other members of the production staff. If the choreographer takes a creative approach to some of the dance sequences resulting in rearrangement, it will require an understanding and tolerant musical director.

Even if the dance numbers are performed as written, close association is necessary for the correct tempo, sight cues, entrances and exits, time changes, and pit sound effects. Any changes the choreographer makes in the score should be done through the musical director, even though the rehearsal pianist notes them on his copy of the score. Also, if the musical director makes necessary cuttings or changes in the dance music, he should inform the choreographer of the changes as soon as possible so dances can be planned accordingly.

Musical bridges between scenes and underscoring often are important to the director if they tie in with change of scene or other stage action. The musical director should list these occasions for the director so he can mark his script accordingly.

In high-school productions the musical director is often the stage director or overall creative head. Whether this practice is due to choice or lack of qualified personnel, it should be discouraged for two main reasons:

1) Stage direction and musical direction are two widely diversified functions. Both require special training. They should artistically compliment each other, not stem from the same source.
2) Both are full-time functions, mainly with different groups. Simultaneous rehearsals are drastically limited. The physical capacity of one man's time and energy can never measure up to one man in each post.

The Choral Rehearsal

In line with the musical director's overall responsibility for everything musical, he is also in charge of the choral direction for both the principals and the singing chorus. However, it is not at all unusual to have an assistant musical director or choral director to handle this responsibility, especially in shows that have more than the usual amount of musical numbers or an abundance of choral work.

A choirmaster or glee-club director is particularly suited for this job. Having this extra member on the staff contributes favorably to rehearsal flexibility. While the musical director is tied up with the orchestra or one of his other duties, the assistant musical director/choral director can be rehearsing the chorus or lead parts. The specific training of a choral director almost always adds professional polish and is just one more way idle time can be put to use to the advantage of the production.

Sometimes the musical director prepares the instrumentation, and the choral or vocal director prepares the singing. Then, working with the stage director, they weave their efforts into the show. The overall responsibility is still that of the musical director, however.

Conducting the Orchestra

Once the show is set and the first performance is underway, the stage director and choreographer have finished their jobs (except for a few minor verbal corrections or suggestions to the cast), but the musical director's job carries through to the last note of the final perform-

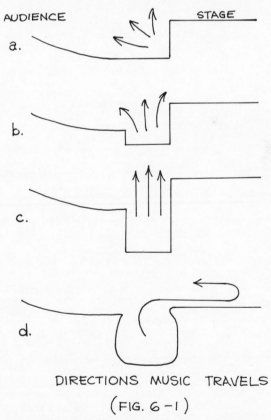

DIRECTIONS MUSIC TRAVELS
(FIG. 6-1)

Knowing how the music travels is important to both cast and audience. Every effort should be made to correct the musical travel to flow to the stage, blend with the voice(s), and then out to the audience as shown in "d." See figure 6-2.

ance. While some professional companies have an additional conductor, the nonprofessional musical director usually inherits the conducting chores. Nonprofessional musicians tend to become dependent on one specific musical director anyway, so there really isn't much choice.

In his duty as conductor, the musical director is largely responsible for pacing each performance. There are about twenty numbers in the average modern musical show. Add the inter-scene music, plus other underscoring (music under dramatic action), and you have a lot of music cues. If each cue is just a few seconds late, it is possible to add several detracting minutes to the show. In theory, the stage manager should cue the orchestra, but in many cases the musical director is in a much better position to do so. Therefore it is wise for the stage manager and musical director to get together and arrange who will cue certain segments of the musical coordination. Whenever the musical director has the best chance, he should pick up his own cue.

Once the singers and dancers achieve basic skill in their musical numbers, the musical director should drill for the precise tempo set by himself or the choreographer. During actual performances, however, nonprofessionals tend to speed things up a little. If, or when, this happens the musical director must yield to the performers on stage in order to keep the mistakes as unobtrusive as possible.

The musical director is also responsible for the overall *sound* of the production. Professionally trained voices are much stronger than amateur voices. The size of the chorus determines what it can sing: fewer voices must sing fewer parts (maybe in unison). Some orchestras have greater dynamic range and can play with more power and yet remain soft enough for the singers to be easily heard. The orchestra has its solos, the overture, dance music, interludes, etc., when it can play stronger and louder, and all this must be coordinated.

Another big factor in this coordination is the pit construction. When there is no pit the sound goes straight up in the air and toward the audience. When a pit exists the sound

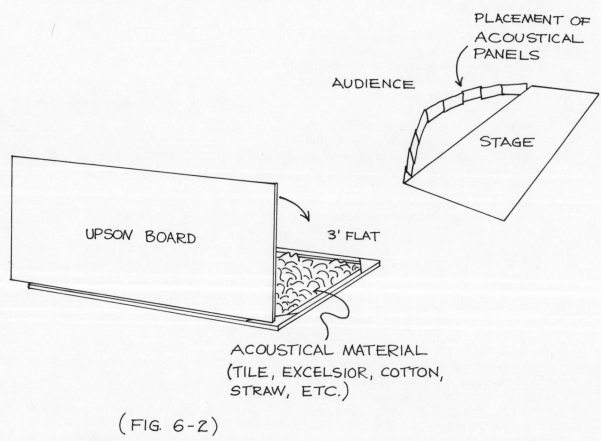

(FIG. 6-2)

Baffle construction and placement to help direct music flow more to stage and then to audience.

South Pacific *at Hill Country Arts Foundation, Ingram, Texas, directed by Julien R. Hughes.*

goes partly to the audience and partly to the stage. When the pit is too deep the sound is muffled and goes straight up in the air. The ideal recessed pit throws the sound up on the stage and then out to the audience.

This is why people on the stage say they can't hear the beat or the melody, and why some people in the audience think the orchestra is too loud. Of course, you can't rebuild the pit, but you can take measures to make the sound more comfortable for all.

If your pit is too deep, construct risers or raised platforms. If the orchestra is just playing in front of the stage, construct a pit "baffle" or front to reflect some of the sound up on the stage. Use cardboard, if nothing else, and paint it to blend in with the set. Better still, use half-size flats (about 3½ feet high when lying on their side) canvas side out. Pack acoustical material behind the canvas and seal shut with a piece of upson board.

There is also a growing tendency to put the orchestra on stage. The split orchestra of *Man of La Mancha* (with half on each side of the main playing area), the hidden orchestra of *I Do! I Do!*, and the various musicians roaming around the stage in *No Strings* are each unique forms of this general idea. The total effect musically is slightly more even as far as the general audience is concerned; however, many complain of a loss of presence. Many performers also claim that it is more difficult to hear the music when it is behind them on stage. The extensive sound system used in the Broadway production of *I Do! I Do!* seemed to hold the best solution to these problems.

"Overtones"

If you've ever read a review of a Broadway musical, you know that the critics usually mention the performers, the producer, the director, the choreographer, the set designer, the costumer—just about everybody but the musical director. Yet, if anything seems the slightest bit wrong with the music or the singing he's in trouble. The professional musical director starts the show off when he steps into the overture spotlight, and his evening isn't over until he collects the musical scores after the orchestra leaves the pit.

The musical director in nonprofessional musical comedy production is called on for much more than is required of a pro, without the money or prestige that go with a professional job. Without his direction and cooperation there would be no musical production. The advancement of the whole nonprofessional musical production movement is more dependent on these men than any other group. To have a good musical director is indeed to be blessed.

CHAPTER VII Settings

*"But Mommy, He Doesn't Look
Like Santa Claus!"*

Santa Claus has become one of the most widely accepted symbols in America. He is found just about everywhere during the Christmas season. For many people, he *is* the Christmas season. The commercialism of Christ's birthday and Santa Claus is somewhat tragic, but it serves to prove a point.

These days it seems every business has a Santa Claus to lure the kiddies in for Christmas cheer and their parents in to spend a few Christmas dollars. The disturbing fact is that these Santas vary widely in quality. They range from top department store Santas to the hucksters in red suits with matted cotton beards so shabby even the youngest children find it difficult to believe that what they are seeing matches their vision of this jolly old man. Nevertheless, all are Santa Clauses. In the quality Santas is found the spirit and joy of the season, as it was meant to be. In the cheap imitations there is a void. Some people say to themselves, "If they were going to do it, why didn't they do it right?"

Stage settings to a musical are as important as Santa Claus is to Christmas. They help establish the time and location of the action. In an interesting way they provide a workable "playground" on which the director and choreographer can move their characters. And in the case of multiscene musicals, set-handling plays a vital role in the correct pacing of the production.

THE SET DESIGNER

Every scenic designer should follow two guidelines before he ever touches pencil to paper to lay out any musical settings. First, read the script thoroughly. Second, read the script again. Reading just the set description at the beginning of each scene is likely to be misleading. Without reading the script, the designer won't get the proper feel of the production and how the sets *must* flow. Many sets used in musicals are not full stage-size sets. Misinterpretation of scene description can cause many handling problems when it is too late to do anything about them.

After the scenic designer has formed the correct set-change sequence, he should make some basic decisions as to the size of each set. At all times he should keep in mind the action that must take place within his creations. Most dance numbers require a lot of room. If there will be numerous people on-stage, there must be enough open space or places within the set to accommodate them. When just a few people are playing a scene or doing a musical number it may be done in an "insert" set or in front of a drop. Drops are also written into many shows to allow for a set change. Keeping all this in mind, the scenic designer should make his first rough sketches of how he thinks the sets should look. The important fact is: The scenic designer should not try to design *anything* without knowing the "flow of the show" and when he does start placing his ideas on paper he *must not strive for the final design.* Just as the sets are built step by step, so must be the designs.

When the first skeleton sketches are completed it is time to research the sets. Record album jackets, programs from the show, magazines, etc., offer valuable *suggestions* on how the set should appear. The sketches are also presented to the production staff, who will usually volunteer a little "research" of their own. The results of these research methods give the scenic designer the ideas and requirements he needs to proceed properly into his "final" designs. Even these finals will have to undergo the scrutiny of the production staff, with changes likely.

Instead of starting right out to limit the designer's thinking or to waste a lot of time coming up with numerous designs, build set designs on the needs of the production flow. This creative process will make for tighter construction and more workable sets because the problem of trying to revise a premature "finished" set design is avoided.

L'il Abner, *directed by Beverly Liebenstein at Kellogg High School, St. Paul, Minnesota, offers an example of a dimensional set in the style of the show not restricted by boxy flats.*

Once the final designs have been approved, usually a few weeks before rehearsals start, blueprints or scale drawings should be prepared. Anyone can be useful in building and painting sets, but they must have *exact* directions to go by. When a diagram says cut a board 6'-6", most people can cut a board 6'-6". When a group is handed a water color sketch and told to build, communications fall flat. Even if the scenic designer is directing the construction and painting, there isn't enough of him to go around. If exact plans for construction are made in advance, individual groups can work on their own. The job will be done faster. Materials are not likely to run short, thanks to the exactness of the pre-planning. Too often nonprofessional sets aren't designed in detail until they are being built— and they look it. Too much depends on sets. They should not be left to just "turn out."

GOOD SETS ARE A MUST

There's an old one-line joke that goes, "If you can't afford Roman candles, blow lightning bugs through a beanshooter." Whereas there may be some similarity in the action taking place in this slogan, there is a decided difference in the results. A Roman candle emits its spectacle with fire and brilliance. Fireflies through a beanshooter are, at best, a poor substitute.

Musicals are more visual than plays. Most rely on spectacular settings to convey their excitement, period, and place in time. In musicals there are more outdoor settings and larger-scale panoramas. Sets that are poor substitutes detract from the performing talent and quality of the orchestra. When the scene changes don't flow without stopping the natural movement of the show, the show drags. Unnecessary time is thus inserted into a production that is normally longer than a play anyway. The "books" of most musicals cannot stand this extra time. It makes the audience restless and causes the show to seem something less than it really is: lightning bugs through a beanshooter instead of the fire of a Roman candle, which most musicals really need.

A New Outlook on Sets

Sets for a one-, two-, or three-act play have been known to cause a lot of difficulty in the past. Now a group can come face to face with musicals that could have as many as 15 or 20 separate settings. How can a group that found it difficult to produce just one set for a play manage to produce the 10 or so better-quality sets required in the average musical? The means vary, but the basic formula stands firm: you do it a lot differently from doing sets for a play.

There is one dogma that bears mentioning at this time. Many groups feel they must build a "library" of scenery. Basically there is nothing wrong with this thinking. It saves money in future years, *if* it can ever be put to use. Where it falls flat is when the current production is inhibited by what a piece of scenery will be good for in the future. Don't save for the future; spend a few extra dollars in doing it right now. Let the larger audiences of the future pick up the slack.

The most disheartening thing that came to light in the Musical Comedy Production Questionnaire was that most groups were still tied to the traditional scenic flats. Flats still have some limited uses in musical scenery, but for the most part the standard unit should be replaced by other materials and different production techniques. Some sets and many professional drops are available from rental firms at a fraction of the cost (time and money) required for the group to make them. Many hours are spent painting certain objects on flats when it would be a lot better and faster to use the actual object. Explanation of these and many other principles of better sets will be discussed later in this chapter, but first it is important to see how and why a different approach is possible.

Set changes in a musical must be made fast. As was mentioned earlier, the fact that they be made fast is basic to the pace and construction of most musicals. There are two main ways of achieving this result: the set-drop sequence and the mechanical stage. The set-drop sequence idea is one in which scene A is played on a full stage set. At the conclusion of scene A, a drop is lowered in front of it. While scene B is being played in front of the drop, the stagehands are tearing down the scene A set in back and replacing it with the set for scene C. Variations on this basic formula are many. For example, there may be a drop plus another set. Or the lights could black out over interlude music while another set is lowered from the fly gallery or pushed in from the wings. When a mechanical stage is employed, however, all the scene changes can be made in full view of the audience.

The Ground Work

Since the tremendous success of the twin revolving turntables used in *My Fair Lady* in 1956, the original version of most modern musicals have used some sort of mechanical stages. Whether these techniques were developed as creative advances for the musical stage, pure need, or the desire to hold down the number of high-priced union stagehands is not really clear. What is clear is that these techniques have become an integral part of many musicals and must be contended with in nonprofessional productions.

Scenery for a nonprofessional musical production must be more portable and self-standing than similar sets for a play. Many sets that would normally be constructed of flats must be executed in some other way. The best way to build anything is to start at the foundation, the very ground (or stage) the sets must stand and often move on.

There are a variety of mechanical stages. The Broadway versions are motor- or wench-driven. They are built to last for years in the event the show is a smash hit. Some are vital to the show; others just make the show run more smoothly.

When one production of *My Fair Lady* went on the road, it employed one set of scenery and two portable stage floors. The twin turntable floor took nearly 2½ days to break down or assemble. The show would play one week in each town. While it was playing in one town the second revolving stage was being dismantled in the preceding town and moved to the town the company would play the following week. Erection would usually be finished just in time for the arrival of the scenery and another week's run. Not only was there the extra expense of two portable stage floors, the extra crew, and moving expense, but the extra week's theatre rent for tying up the stage preceding the show when the turntables were being set up and the time after the show when the alternate was being

Two unique solutions to the multi-set problem. How to Succeed in Business Without Really Trying, *produced by Brigham Young University, Provo, Utah, Max Golightly, director; Charles Henson, designer; and* West Side Story, *produced by the Chanticleer*

dismantled. This procedure cost a lot of money, a factor in which the producer has more than a casual interest. Yet he considered it so important to his show that no expense was spared to do the job right.

Naturally, nonprofessional groups cannot come anywhere near the costs involved in building one of these professional sub-stages, but they can achieve the same function at a fraction of the cost. The ideal run for most nonprofessional musical productions is two weekends. It's rarely that the scenery must be transported from one location to another. Whereas the professional must think in terms of years, steel, rails, cable, and theatre adaptability, non-pro groups are only concerned with days, wood, cheap rubber casters, rope, and one theatre.

The foundation or groundwork is largely one of licking the problems created by musicals written to be performed on a mechanical

stage, i.e., substituting less expensive methods to achieve the same results. The following are a few practical items nonprofessional groups can use to make their musicals flow more smoothly:

1) The Turntable
2) Tracked floors
3) Wagons
4) Knives
5) Portable set units
6) Side stages
7) Insert sets
8) Stick sets

THE TURNTABLE

Turntables have many uses in musical productions, both on stage and off. They may or may not be round. Most Broadway turntables are round because they are built into a subfloor.

Players, Council Bluffs, Iowa, Norman Filbert, director. Building all scenic require-ments into one set, however, cuts down the intimacy and focal attention of the audience —and, of course, requires a larger stage.   BOB PYLES STUDIO

Nonprofessional groups may duplicate turn-tables in a variety of forms. What makes it a turntable is a central pivot point. Here again a variety of devices may be used for this pivot point, but the easiest method is just to use a 1″ pipe, pipe stand, and a hole slightly larger (about 1¼″) in the turntable platform. The turntable platform rests on 6 to 10 casters mounted at right angles to the center hole and forming a circumference around it. The platform itself (1″ or ¾″ plywood with 2″ x 4″ framing) can be constructed of several smaller sections bolted together with large stove bolts. Power to move the turntable can be supplied by rope, cable, hook, or actors onstage. One motorized caster will do the job, too, but the price for these is still out of the range of most groups.

Long hook handles, like those shown in Figure 7-3, are used to hook into steel rings at the side of the turntable (near the corners for greater leverage if the platform has any right angles). If sets are mounted solidly on the turntable platform, the actors (or costumed stagehands) can push to revolve it as part of the action.

The turntable can be sectioned off at the middle through the pivot point or offset several feet giving the effect that one side is shallow and the other side deep.

There is something professional in seeing the stage go around, and it is an easy effect to achieve when it is prefabricated in sections and the means to power it are kept simple.

WAGON

A wagon is nothing more than a raised platform on recessed wheels or casters. Usually the wagon is a square or rectangular platform on which different sets can be mounted during the performance. It can usually be pushed into position from the wings or to an upstage posi-

(FIG. 7-1) TURNTABLES

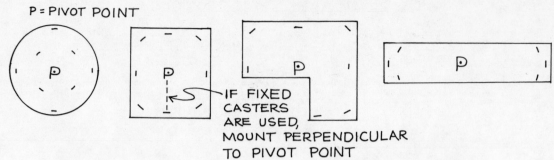

P = PIVOT POINT

IF FIXED
CASTERS
ARE USED,
MOUNT PERPENDICULAR
TO PIVOT POINT

Turntables are best used to move major scenes or those requiring second levels and/or a lot of furniture quickly into place.

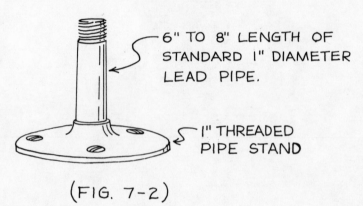

6" TO 8" LENGTH OF
STANDARD 1" DIAMETER
LEAD PIPE.

1" THREADED
PIPE STAND

(FIG. 7-2)

Standard lead pipe fittings used to make a turntable pivot.

6 TO 8' LONG

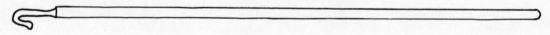

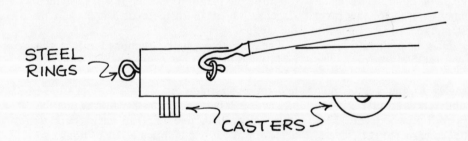

STEEL
RINGS

CASTERS

ROTATING TURNTABLES
(FIG. 7-3)

Usually turntables can be rotated by stagehands, costumed if necessary. If it is desired to keep this rotation power hidden, removable rope pulls or modified window opening handles can be used.

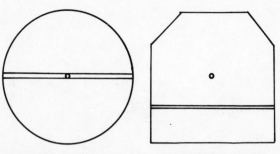

STANDARD SPLIT
TURNTABLE

DOWNSTAGE
PARTITION GAINS
LARGER STAGE
AREA ON REVOLVE

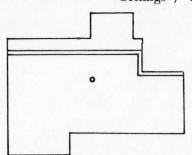

HOUSE TURNTABLE
EXTERIOR &
INTERIOR

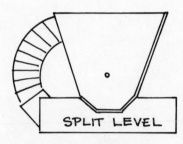

SPLIT LEVEL

SPECIAL PURPOSE UNIT
WITH STEPS

(FIG. 7-4)

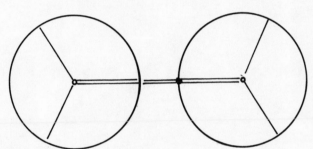

DOUBLE TURNTABLES—DIVIDED
INTO THREE SECTIONS AS USED
IN THE ORIGINAL PRODUCTION
OF "MY FAIR LADY"

TYPES OF TURNTABLES

The versatility of turntables is really unlimited. Here are a few modifications to spark the imagination.

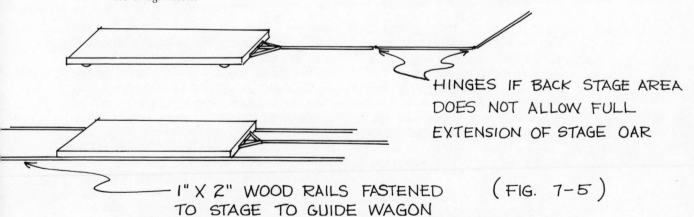

HINGES IF BACK STAGE AREA
DOES NOT ALLOW FULL
EXTENSION OF STAGE OAR

1" X 2" WOOD RAILS FASTENED
TO STAGE TO GUIDE WAGON

(FIG. 7-5)

Wagons are highly versatile as they can be used as the basis for portable set pieces or just furnishings anywhere onstage. They are particularly valuable for use from the downstage wings. Wagons over 16' wide are usually introduced from an upstage storage area behind the last drop and moved to a center or downstage playing area.

Dimensional upson board set pieces for Dayton Summer Theatre production of **The Music Man.** *Note the cut-out details.*

tion behind a backdrop. It is pushed into position by means of a stage oar. If extreme accuracy is desired on a regular stage, 1″ x 2″ guide rails can be nailed into the stage.

If a wagon is to be much longer than 8 feet, it should be built in two or more sections and connected with pin hinges with special easily removable pins for quick backstage dismantling as they come offstage. Smaller pin hinges are also useful for attaching sets to wagons, turntables, etc.

TRACKED FLOORS

A change in scenery for a play is usually marked on the stage floor with tape or paint. When a scene is set up the stage crew double-checks to see that everything is "on the marks." In musicals some scenes must slide on in their exact position in a matter of seconds. The best system for achieving this precision is a tracked or slotted stage floor.

This system requires that the entire operating stage floor be covered with 1″ plywood for elevation and then topped with Masonite for hardness. By leaving ¾″ gaps between certain sections (allowing the permanent stage floor to show through) tracks or slots are created for guiding portable scenery.

There are two types of hardware for mounting the portable set pieces: a round pin for moving up- and downstage and a 3″-wide steel cleat for lateral moving units.

Units moving down- and upstage require at least two tracks for proper control. With this type of sub-floor all the power is supplied by stagehands walking behind the set piece.

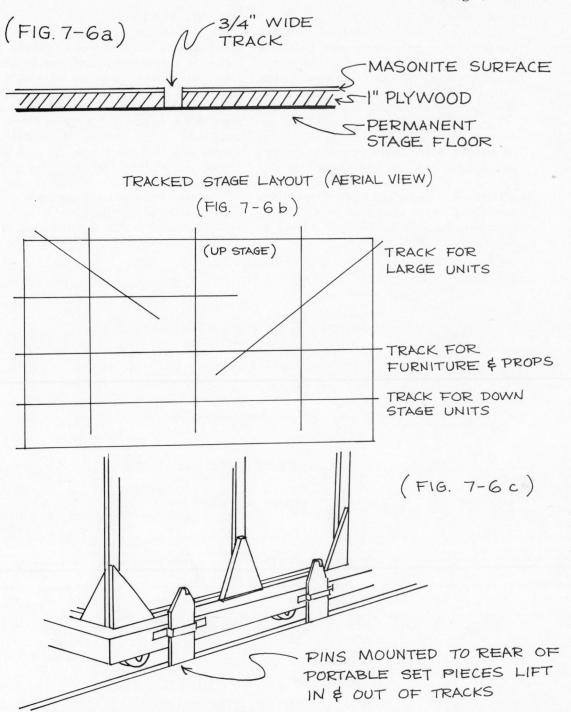

(FIG. 7-6a)

3/4" WIDE TRACK

MASONITE SURFACE

1" PLYWOOD

PERMANENT STAGE FLOOR

TRACKED STAGE LAYOUT (AERIAL VIEW)

(FIG. 7-6 b)

(UP STAGE)

TRACK FOR LARGE UNITS

TRACK FOR FURNITURE & PROPS

TRACK FOR DOWN STAGE UNITS

(FIG. 7-6 c)

PINS MOUNTED TO REAR OF PORTABLE SET PIECES LIFT IN & OUT OF TRACKS

One of the easiest mechanical stage systems to achieve is the tracked or slotted stage . . . just as they are used in many Broadway productions. To employ the system, 1″ plywood is nailed to the existing stage floor leaving a series of ¾″ gaps between certain sections (a) thereby forming recessed guides for wagons and other portable set pieces. Duplicate sections of Masonite are nailed to the plywood to create a hard surface. The number of tracks required vary to each production, however; the three main uses are from the downstage wings horizontally across the stage; from upstage wings to down center stage; and from upstage behind a drop straight down stage. (b). Removable guiding hardware is mounted on each portable unit . . . ½″ round pins (not shown) for upstage-downstage movement and 3″ wide steel cleats for stage right-stage left movements (c).

KNIFE SETS

The knife is another movable platform that swings on from an offstage area. It is in a fixed position on- and offstage. It can be pie-shaped, circular, or square. Its main feature is that it swings from a pivot point at the corner or edge of the platform.

The main disadvantages with knives is that they need a lot of room to swing on (if they are any size at all), and they can be cumbersome fixed in the wings. Knives with a movable pivot point can offer extra flexibility, but are still difficult to handle and block a lot of other possibilities. But in some cases in which wing space does not allow for a wagon, a knife arrangement can work well.

PORTABLE SET UNITS

Portable set units are similar to other movable platforms, but though other movable platforms can accommodate several sets at different times during the production, the portable set unit is built as a unit and must stay that way. For example, a portable set unit could be a show wagon in *Carnival,* a rolling flat like the ones used in *No Strings,* Nellie Forbush's shower stall in *South Pacific,* or the portable towers used to form various settings in *Pickwick.* They are built as a special purpose unit and remain intact (except for some folding here and there so everything can fit backstage). Other examples include the train from *Hello, Dolly!,* the bridge from *Brigadoon,* the old-

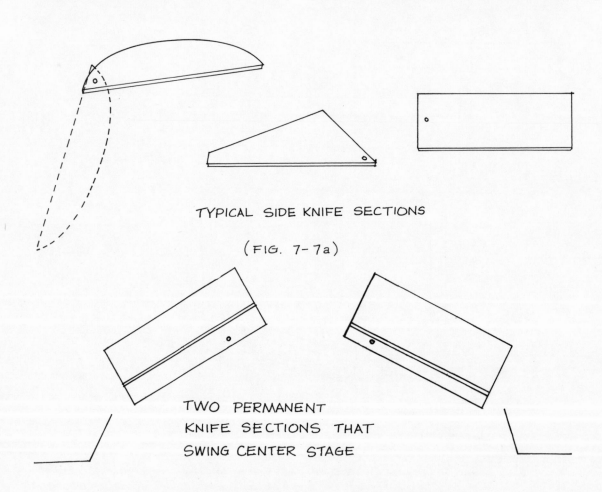

TYPICAL SIDE KNIFE SECTIONS

(FIG. 7-7a)

TWO PERMANENT
KNIFE SECTIONS THAT
SWING CENTER STAGE

(FIG. 7-7b)

Knife platforms are somewhat a cross between a wagon and a turntable. They are semi-fixed movable platforms with an eccentric pivot point (a). They can swing on and offstage or offer sufficient versatility to remain onstage permanently. Two large knife sections, with different mask inserts, can accommodate three major full-stage settings (b). The complete scenic requirements of some shows can be handled with a full stage knife arrangement (c).

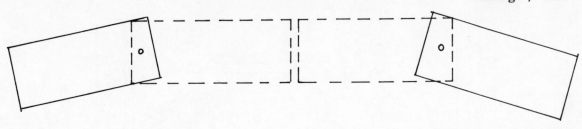

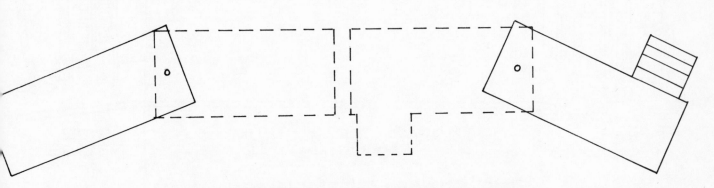

FULL STAGE KNIFE ARRANGEMENT
(FIG. 7-7c)

time car from *Good News* and the Pullman car interior used in *The Music Man*. For one reason or another all these sets must be moved in or out of position quickly. Their place in the show is vital to a musical number or the pace of the show. They aren't necessarily built on platforms, but their superstructure is mounted on wheels or casters that are usually hidden.

SIDE STAGES

Where the main stage or wing space is too small to accommodate all the necessary settings, some consideration should be given to the use of side stages. These are small, shallow playing areas built out in the house or regular audience section, on one or both sides of the proscenium arch. They should be angled slightly toward the center of the house and used only for intimate scenes that include only a few people. They are ideal for small recurring scenes, love scenes, solos, etc. They are of no value for dance numbers, choral numbers, or scenes in which there is a lot of action.

Side stages can contribute very favorably to the mood-creating decor of the theatre and enhance the production while they are really covering up for lack of facilities.

Entrances and exits to side stages can be made from the proscenium arch or through the audience.

INSERT SETS

An insert set is an independent set that can be used in two ways. 1) as part of a larger set: for example, a front porch that couples with a house drop. The painted house completes the scene and masks a set change going on behind it, but all the action takes place in the general area of the porch. 2) as a portable set unit inserted into a larger set that is used for a different purpose. For example, *South Pacific* has various office and hideaway scenes that could well be played on insert sets in front of the elaborate South Seas exteriors required in other scenes. Since *South Pacific* is a set-drop-set show, this also eliminates excess scenery and tightens the construction of the show. The only requirement for an insert set is that it provide enough room to play the scene. A drop may be flown in to mask the remainder of the main set or it can be faded into darkness by concentrating lights on the insert set.

STICK SETS

Stylized "stick" or impressionistic sets have their place in the musical theatre as long as

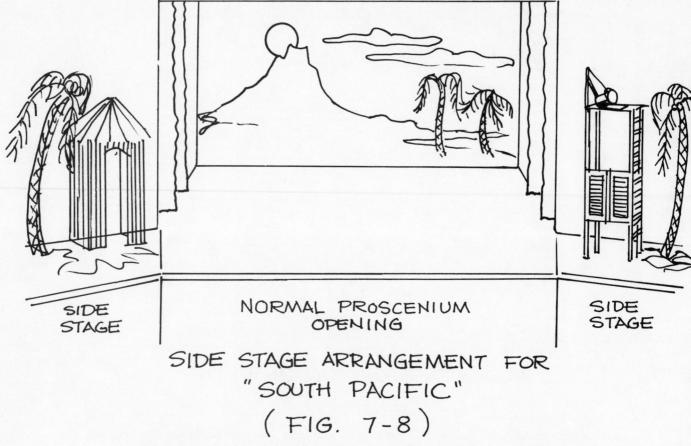

SIDE STAGE ARRANGEMENT FOR "SOUTH PACIFIC"
(FIG. 7-8)

Side stages are extensions built out into the house at either or both sides of the proscenium arch. They are most valuable for intimate or recurring scenes involving only a few people.

they are effective. They should never be an excuse for what should have been. Stick sets are a necessity for arena, in-the-round, and some three-quarter productions. Other than that they should be avoided. As was mentioned earlier, the spectacle of full-blown sets are part of musical production. Most nonprofessional audiences find it difficult to accept even the most imaginative skeletons.

Realistic settings also pick up the amateur performer and help him get into the mood of the show—and make it easier for him to portray his part. He need not concentrate on imagining anything but the role he is playing. It pays to know your precise set and scenic-drop needs well in advance.

AERIAL WORKS

In addition to the procedures outlined for use on the ground or stage level, there are certain alternatives from aerial positions. Recommended possibilities are:

1) Sets that fly
2) Projected scenery
3) Lighting techniques
4) Legs, drops, and travelers

SETS THAT FLY

One of the fastest ways to get a set into position is to lower it from the fly gallery. This still leaves the problem of getting furniture and props into their proper place, but it does accomplish the bulk of the job of getting a set into place. Many kinds of sets can be flown in. Flats, set pieces (such as posts, columns, arches, signs), or entire interior sets, to name only a few. Stranded piano wire is attached at the base of the set to be flown, *not at the top*. The wire is threaded through hook eyes, two or three others placed on the back of the set (depending on its height).

This way the weight of the set keeps everything perpendicular, whereas when wires are attached at the top of the set, they "fly in" on

(FIG. 7-9)

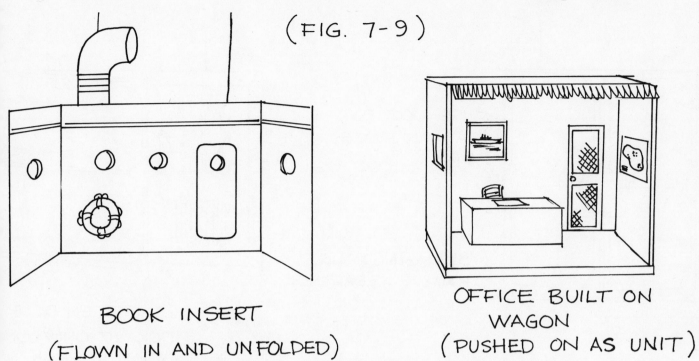

BOOK INSERT

(FLOWN IN AND UNFOLDED)

OFFICE BUILT ON
WAGON

(PUSHED ON AS UNIT)

Short scenes in most musicals are played in front of a drop or in a small insert setting. These inserts are usually flown in center stage or pushed into view from either downstage wing.

(FIG. 7-10)

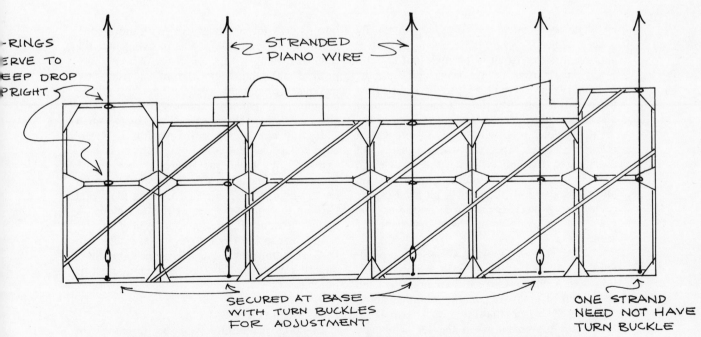

Rear view of a row of buildings to be used before a skydrop. Flats are joined together by 1″ x 3″s. Stranded piano wire is threaded through screw eyes or steel O-rings and attached to base of the unit. All but one line includes turnbuckle for fine adjustment after all fly wires are attached to batten.

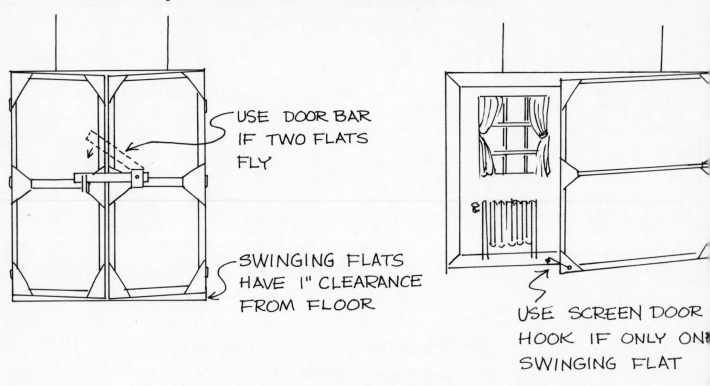

USE DOOR BAR IF TWO FLATS FLY

SWINGING FLATS HAVE 1" CLEARANCE FROM FLOOR

USE SCREEN DOOR HOOK IF ONLY ONE SWINGING FLAT

(FIG. 7-11)

Sets that fly must be secure. Use a bar for two folding panels, a regular screen door hook at the base for one panel. Swinging panels should have ½" to 1" floor clearance for easy setup.

an angle and tend to get fouled up in the fly gallery. The wires are strung to a batten, making sure the batten will remain out of sight when the set rests on the stage and that the bottom of the set will be out of sight when the batten is raised to the rafters. The number of wires required depends on the width of the set to be flown; one wire every 8 feet, with a minimum of two wires, will work in just about every case. It is difficult to get the wires even, so it is wise to use adjustable turnbuckles on all but one wire, so the set will hit level on the stage. This protects the set from hitting on one point and breaking or otherwise damaging the scene.

Folding sets or "book flats" pose few problems in "flying in." They fly in a closed position with a standard screen door hook to keep them shut. The "flap" panel is mounted about ¾" to 1" higher than the back panels to allow free movement when the set is opened and closed.

PROJECTED SCENERY

The field for projected scenery has been around for a long time, but is just coming into its own for practical use. With more common use the equipment is improving and the price is coming within the range of some non-professional groups. Both front and rear projections can create realistic outdoor backgrounds, sky patterns, thunderstorms, moving clouds, slums, skyscrapers—all from small slides and one backdrop or cyclorama. Reference to special books on this subject is suggested if this technique interests your group. Preparation of slides, operation of the equipment, and special controlled lighting play vital parts in the successful use of this technique. A certain amount of experimentation may be necessary before the desired results are achieved. It is recommended that all aspects be thoroughly investigated before any equipment is purchased.

LIGHTING TECHNIQUES

Lighting techniques will be discussed in greater detail in Chapter IX. Mention here refers to how lighting can be used to illuminate special areas of the stage. Professionally this is accomplished by groups of lights trained to light the specific area and may not have any other use in the entire show. Most nonprofessional groups cannot afford this type of luxury and must rely on follow spots to do the job.

This technique lends itself more to impressionistic productions than to realistic ones and can fall flat if done poorly. It usually requires a certain amount of extra lighting equipment and a patient person with more than casual experience with lighting systems.

This method is completely useless in a theatre in which a blackout cannot be achieved. Theatres with white walls, windows, bright exit signs, or too much light from the orchestra pit can ruin the effect and detract from the show.

Legs, Drops, and Travelers

When most nonprofessional groups think of flying in sets, they automatically think of drops. Too few groups use legs or devise creative applications for travelers.

Legs. Legs, for those who may not be familiar with the term, are the masking panels at the extreme sides of the stage. They may be painted a solid color or carry out the decor or atmosphere of the production. Instead of being panels they could be houses, buildings, lattice work, trees, columns, etc. Usually they are flown, but they could be pushed on from the wings. Legs eliminate the use of regular drapes as masking. (Exposed auditorium curtains are a definite trademark of an amateur musical production.) Three legs on each side of the stage would be enough for the largest stages. Two would be adequate for smaller ones.

Travelers. Traveler curtains are used in most nonprofessional theatres for their main curtain. These travelers convey two half curtains to a center point, closing the stage to the audience's view. Special traveler equipment is available to perform other functions. These special units can travel a curtain from offstage in one direction along the entire length of the rod. Such travelers open new avenues for theatres without fly gallery. Special drops and painted drapes can be used with these travelers to achieve interesting effects and provide flexibility not possible before.

Other special travelers allow the use of single-piece drapes two or three times the width of the proscenium opening. When traveled across the stage from beginning to end they provide a moving background for stationary actors, cars, trains, etc.

Drops. The use of painted drops is a must in most musicals. A plain light-blue sky drop is a basic investment for any group doing musical productions. This versatile drop can be adapted with various types of ground rows (set pieces along the base of the drop) to fit just about any situation.

The use of scrims or gauze drops is always a good effect to dissolve from one scene into another. When lit from in front, what is painted on the scrim is seen by the audience. When lights are turned on behind it, the scrim becomes invisible. Scrim material can also be used as part of set panels or stretched over framing to make entire sets.

In lieu of renting, many standard or even special drops can be purchased from scenery companies, but if a workshop area is available it is always cheaper for the group to paint their own. Painting techniques will be discussed later, but here it should be mentioned that drops should be painted on a flat surface. A gymnasium-size floor or perhaps a large stage floor are best suited for this purpose. Care must be taken to have a leakproof tarpaulin or polyethylene dropcloth under the drop to be painted. This prevents seeping paint from marring the floor's surface.

Muslin or light canvas may be sewn together to make the drop, or the complete unpainted drop may be purchased from a scenic supply house. Most home sewing machines are not designed to take heavy drop materials, and it is difficult to handle hundreds of yards of material on such equipment. Chances are a commercial drapery shop or upholsterer would be able to do the job. If the job is to be done by hand (which is often the best), the sections to be joined should be matched up end to end on a rounded surface about 4″ high (a rug roll or large mailing tube is ideal.) Stitching is easier than if done on a flat surface; it will be more even, and the drop will hang straighter without wrinkles.

Drops made of kraft wrapping paper in vertical strips connected with paper tape have been used on some occasions with some impressive results. This allows cutout drops without ruining expensive materials. Seamless paper, which is available from most advertising display companies or suppliers, is even better for this purpose. Weight battens for both methods must be carefully chosen.

Set Materials

Musicals require a fast-paced production. To meet this requirement, sets must be streamlined with new construction techniques and materials to do a bigger job faster. For the most part, good old flats have to go.

Instead, use *upson* board, a paper building material, available from any lumberyard. It comes in standard 4′ x 8′ sheets and a variety of thicknesses. Cut outlines, window openings, skylines, lattice work, arches, etc. Form columns, beams, and statues. Add dimension instead of using boxy-looking flats. Upson board tacks easily to a wood frame and does not require any stretching or sizing coat. Use a "Cutawl" cutting tool to cut the most intricate design or to lop off a big hunk of board. Electric jigsaws will also do the job, but they leave a rough edge. Upson board can also be pieced for large panels without a trace.

Other than upson board, the local lumberyard is full of exciting new budget building materials ideal for set construction. Some examples are veneered paneling, tiles, contact paper, decorative posts, railing, door frames, hardware items, brick paper, trims, etc. Using the actual item saves valuable time in set construction, is unquestionably more effective, and many times is no more expensive than using standard set materials.

Seamless display paper comes in many colors and can offer prepainted sets merely by stapling it to wood frames. Staple it to the edge of the frame so the staples will not reflect stage lighting. Use it to form cycloramas or a lightweight ceiling. Fix it to the back wall for an extra drop.

Burlap, netting, fireproof display satin, and other yard goods are surprisingly cheap when purchased from wholesale outlets. Never try to paint cloth on a set, use the real thing. Use polyethylene for clear windows.

Use "seed" lights (small Christmas lights) for neon signs, stars in a drop, spelling out the name of the show during the overture, in nightclub scenes, or wherever they wouldn't be completely out of place.

Other interesting set materials mentioned in the Musical Comedy Production Questionnaire included the following:

pre-fab sets
plastics
bamboo
large portable murals
wallpaper
wide ribbons
Masonite
war surplus materials
carpeting
tobacco cloth
aluminum frames
pressed board

Of course, there are still some instances in which flats are the most desirable, but these are becoming few and far between.

The Broadway production of *Mr. President* exemplified professional search for new set materials. The scenery incorporated 84 electromagnets to hold various set pieces together. Basic wall units would be transformed into just about anything by the flip of a few switches and the right decorator pieces. One powerful magnet could hold everything from a large presidential emblem to a bed canopy to a revolving shooting gallery target.

Imagination among nonprofessional groups can lead to new and wonderfully exciting materials and sets, realistic sets that will please the audience and add immeasurably to any musical production. Musical theatre grew up on splendor, glamour, and lavish productions. Today it is easy to supply all three for a surprisingly low cost. It's time every director and set designer found out all the advantages of the creative use of new materials.

Set Paintings

Professional sets, for the most part, are dyed, not painted. There are a lot of advantages in using dyes, particularly if they must last a long time or be moved around a lot. Scenic dyes can be very difficult to work with —almost impossible if you have no idea of what you are doing. Their use isn't really necessary for nonprofessional productions. Even old glue-base powdered paints aren't worth the trouble anymore.

Today there are a number of water-base paints, such as Luminal, which come as a concentrated paste in gallon cans. They mix in a flash and dry quickly. (There are also some new one-step powdered paints that claim to offer the same versatility at a lower price.) Properly prepared paste concentrates are ideal for use on scenic panels, cardboard inserts, or drops. Thin them down a little more for painting scrims. Use full strength to highlight scrims.

Painting techniques are important to give style to the production and to get the job done fast. Completely paint the set with the correct flat color (unless you are using a precolored material). Use colored tape or ribbon for thin lines and straight highlights. Carefully paint in any details that MUST be painted. Add any necessary texture by "dry-brushing." Dry-brushing means having just enough paint on the paint brush to give a net-like effect when the brush is lightly stroked over the surface to be painted. This technique gives texture and/or highlights and diffuses harsh lines.

The last step is one used on just about every professional and summer-stock set ever

Ship insert set for The King and I, *staged at Ursuline College, Louisville, Kentucky, directed by Robert M. Fischer.*

built. This is the diffusing technique known to most scenic artists as "spattering." This technique should be considered vital to any non-professional set. Color dots are splattered on the nearly finished set by hitting the flat side of a brush of paint against a board held about four to six feet away from the set or drop being splattered. The more paint in the brush the larger the splatter dots. Black is a good color to splatter, but usually several corresponding colors are used. Splatter heavily in corners for shadows. Splatter for texture and highlights. Splatter to diffuse harsh lines.

Another technique is to paint the set pieces with flat coats of paint and draw in the details with colored chalks. It provides a very interesting and arty effect for period sets or sets with an international flavor. Chalk, of course, will rub off. Prevent this by spraying with an aerosol fixing solution or by spraying clear sizing solution through commercial paint-spraying equipment. The latter can usually be rented from a local equipment rental firm.

Some noteworthy painting shortcuts are: 1) Use a rectangular sponge to paint bricks: Dip brick-size sponge in pan of paints, squeeze out excess paint, and make brick impressions, using the sponge like a rubber stamp. When dry go back over with a coarser sponge and darken or lighten color for highlights; 2) Paint-soaked rags rolled over set panels can create some interesting texture effects. Experimentation is suggested to determine just what can be accomplished; 3) Tree leaves and unusual shadowing effects can be achieved by taking a 1″ or 1½″ brush and various shades of the same color. Saturate the brush with paint. Stipple one side at a time by lifting the brush 2″ to 3″ from the set similar to the use of a stencil brush, but more with the side of the brush rather than the tip. Overlap the different shades. Use in small areas or patches for shadowing. Slightly larger brushes may be used for large areas of tree leaves.

Help for set painting can usually be obtained from high-school or college art students. (The author mentions this point because it works and because this is the way show business got into his blood many years ago.) Housewives also have been observed painting a "mean" set during the daylight hours while hubby is at the office and the kids are in school. But when it comes right down to it, anyone can paint a professional-looking set

An excellent example of impressionistic design. The library scene from The Music Man.

when he has the proper instruction and direction.

DRESSING THE SET

Paint sets with a flat coat of paint. Use the real thing whenever possible. Decorate the set like window displays in department store windows. Real pictures on the walls, "real" artificial flowers, enough furniture, and all the little details that really make a set look authentic. Much of this detail will depend on how the set change will be made, i.e., moving platform, behind a drop with plenty of setup and take-down time, or a quickie change without benefit of a movable platform.

Here again, the use of fabric drapes or panels is recommended. If it's an outdoor scene, use several fly-ins—combinations of painted drops, legs, a ground row, and/or scrim—instead of just one drop. Wherever possible give depth to the set. Logs, straw, dried leaves, and other easily attainable items can really make a world of difference.

Where to get furniture? The same place the group would get furniture for a play. In passing, these could be the Goodwill, Salvation Army, St. Vincent de Paul, or other second-hand shops. Some period pieces, or just about anything, really, can be rented. Many furniture shops or department stores will lend merchandise for an acknowledgment in the program. And then there is each cast member's storage room, garage, and/or attic, plus school storage rooms or warehouses if it's a high-school or college group.

A musical has more furniture and stage props than a play. Sometimes handling all these pieces can create a big problem. Make sure the problems are avoided by carefully planning and making the necessary pieces ready backstage.

SPECIAL PROBLEMS

Every group has to live with *some* problems. Some groups have to live with *impossible*

In the multi-fly method (a) two extra 1" x 3" battens are attached to a drop and all four battens are rigged with ¼" nylon line. Starting with the top, the battens are pulled individually to the ceiling thereby hiding the drop behind the teaser curtain.

In the roll-up method (b) the drop is fixed to the ceiling and the lower batten is rotated to roll up the painted scene.

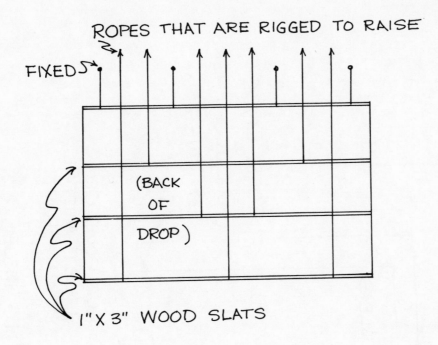

ROPES THAT ARE RIGGED TO RAISE

FIXED

(BACK
OF
DROP)

1" X 3" WOOD SLATS

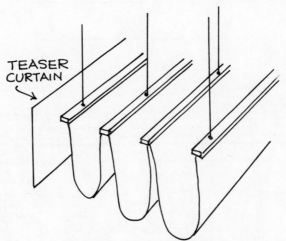

TEASER
CURTAIN

WHEN FLOWN SHOULD LOOK
LIKE THIS FROM ABOVE
AT REAR

(FIG. 7-12a)

MULTI-FLY METHOD FOR FLYING
DROP WITHOUT A FLY GALLERY

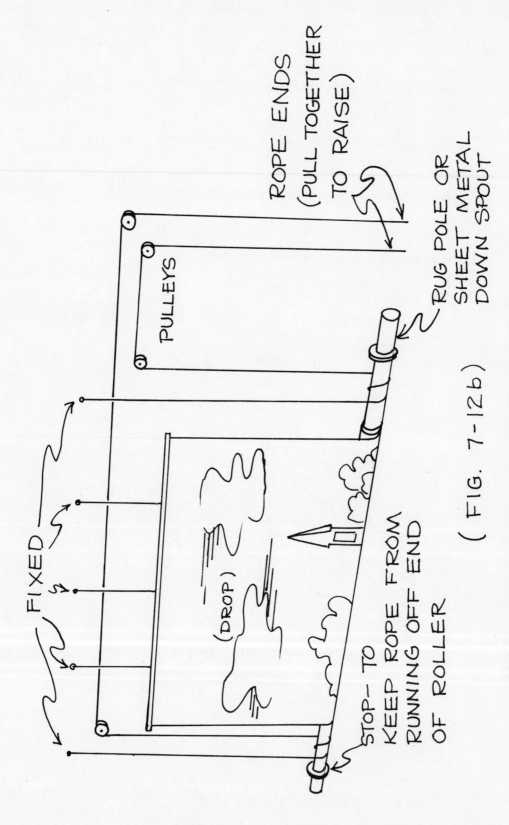

ROPE ENDS
(PULL TOGETHER
TO RAISE)

PULLEYS

RUG POLE OR
SHEET METAL
DOWN SPOUT

FIXED

(DROP)

STOP – TO
KEEP ROPE FROM
RUNNING OFF END
OF ROLLER

(FIG. 7-12b)

ROLL-UP METHOD FOR FLYING DROP
WITHOUT A FLY GALLERY

Leuzinger High School Lawndale, California, production of West Side Story directed by Julien R. Hughes.

Portable set units for Carnival, *produced at J. S. Morton East High School, Cicero, Illinois, Jack L. Leckel, director.*

problems. Three big problems in presenting musicals are: 1) too small a stage; 2) a stage without a fly gallery; 3) a stage that has a tile floor or doubles as a gymnasium.

Stages that are too small were mentioned earlier with the use of side stages. A platform extension at the front of the stage is also a possibility. The best solution is to stick to small shows until new facilities can be built or rented. Sometimes even the use of a movie theatre building would be better than trying to do a large show on a small stage.

Stages without fly galleries are more flexible than small stages, but still have some limitations. Drops can be avoided wherever possible, but there are at least two ways in which they can be used.

Tile and gymnasium floors are poor substitutes for a regular stage floor. (Concrete floors are also rough on dancers.) They can't be nailed into and it is normally difficult to fix pivot points needed for revolving sets. If it is a gymnasium floor, there is a chance it has small metal plates to secure other types of athletic equipment. A pivot pipe welded to an insert plate the size of the existing plate can replace it during the show's run. Large rubber casters won't produce any damaging effects on expensive gym floors.

Staging musicals in the round is a completely different world and very difficult to do. Such problems as where to put the orchestra, controlling the sound, sets, entrances and exits of large groups of people, direction and choreography to the entire audience, give you some idea of what you are up against. Several professional tent and arena companies, however, do an outstanding job of presenting musicals in this manner. Study of one of these operations should be essential to anyone restricted to this technique.

SCENERY RENTALS

From time to time mention has been made of set and drop rentals. In many sections of the country this is a distinct possibility, particularly in respect to drop rentals. Rental charges may range from $15 to $35 per drop, but the time saved and the quality they add are worth the price. Besides, you can't paint a drop for less than that, let alone pay for a pre-fab drop.

A few words of caution, however, should be kept in mind when renting drops or set pieces.

1) If at all possible, see the drops or set pieces you are renting well in advance of the show. Selection from photographs or color slides can often lead to disappointment. The photography may have been done many years back when the settings were new. Age and use may have rendered them useless for a tasteful production. It is worth a special trip to the rental company to make sure the group doesn't get stuck with something they can't or don't want to use.

2) If several drops are to be used, make sure they go together. Artistic painting styles and color tones are as numerous as the artists who painted the settings and the companies who supplied the paint. The differences can be very obvious. Such differences give the production a hodgepodge look. Always look for the rental agent who might own the original drops from the New York or road show companies. When you can, rent all the necessary pieces as a unit; do so rather than trying to pick "suitable" pieces from a variety of sources.

3) Most rental fees do not include shipment or freight charges. Make sure to get a complete estimate on what these charges

will amount to before closing any deal for rented settings. This simple step can mean the difference between profit and loss, should the freight bills become staggering.

A good source to determine the names of companies who rent scenery, drops, and other theatrical materials is the *Simon's Directory of Theatrical Materials, Services and Information.* Every group should have an up-to-date copy of this edition for general reference. If yours doesn't, chances are it is on file at your local library, or the current edition may be obtained from: Package Publicity Service, Inc., 1564 Broadway, New York, N.Y. 10036.

DESIGN FOR SUCCESS

Good sets can't make a musical show, but they surely can help. Bad sets can only detract from a good performance. The average musical has a great many more sets than does the average play. Materials used to build sets for musicals should be different from the old standby flats. Methods for moving sets are essential. In short, a whole new outlook must be given to the problem of sets. Look into it further right now. Don't produce a show that conveys the image of a dirty old man in a red suit and cotton beard. Never cheat your audience. Create an image like unto a full-blown, genuine-looking Santa Claus, one that captures the true spirit and joy of the occasion.

CHAPTER VIII   Costumes and Makeup

"A Thimbleful of Miracles"

The musical *Pins and Needles* opened at the Labor Stage Theatre on November 27, 1937. The cast was made up of members of the International Ladies' Garment Workers' Union, all nonprofessional show people. Furthermore all the production functions were performed by other union members. When *Pins and Needles* closed 1,108 performances later it had become the longest running musical ever to play New York up to that time, second only to the plays, *Abie's Irish Rose* and *Lightnin'* in longevity.

It is a fitting and just paradox that such honor and success should befall the purveyors of needles and thread. For it is these hard-working, often unrewarded souls of today who must bear the terrific burden of costuming the modern musical. The author sympathizes with the problems of costume people and the way their work is judged. That is, if a costume is right it usually goes unnoticed, but if something is wrong about it, the creators catch "suggestions" from the director all the way down to the chorus boy who wears it in a walk-on part. Then there are the girls' mothers who want to remake daughter's costume and add something a "little special." The toil is long, the labor tedious, and the reward unknown. But without costumes, what would any show be?

Next to plays themselves, probably more books are written on costuming than on any other theatrical subject. History of costuming, costume design, costume execution, helpful hints on costuming, and other titles fill several shelves in any library.

Yet the costumes seen in many musicals are a mess.

Why?

There could be many reasons. Sometimes a costume rental house sends poor costumes. Other times homemade costumes don't quite turn out. Most times people just don't plan ahead.

Not too long ago the author received a call from one of the local high schools inquiring where they could get some good costumes for a production of *Guys and Dolls*. When asked when the performance would be, the response came back, "next week." The group had been rehearsing for nine weeks and just naturally assumed they wouldn't have any trouble finding 1930's suits. A short visit to their opening night showed they never did locate what was going to be so easy to find. The broad lapels they did find were much too large. Too bad! All that hard work and then the costumes made the actors look silly. The dancers couldn't move right. The male singing chorus were wearing their own suits.

Just what is a costume? A costume is just as much a part of the characterization as all the weeks of rehearsal necessary to develop the human component. In one of his series of articles in *Dramatics* magazine on staging musicals, Robert W. Ensley says, "costumes are actually an extension of the scenic background." Besides being part of the character and the production's visual effect, a costume must also hold up, allow movement, look authentic, and be functional to the needs of the part. A costume may include props or accessories, i.e., hats, canes, gloves, etc. Wherever an area of confusion could exist, make sure the costume department and prop committee know who is responsible for acquiring each item.

The average full-size musical could easily require at least a hundred costumes. Getting each performer's size, assembling all the necessary costume ensembles, and programming frequent costume changes is a major organization job. The best tool in getting the job done is the scene-by-scene "costume plot" as it relates to each cast member.

When the costume plot has been completed, the costume designer and wardrobe mistress are ready to go to work. To make or to rent, that is the question.

The Musical Comedy Production Questionnaire asked how each group surveyed obtained their costumes. Here are the results:

My Fair Lady, *Ursuline College, Louisville, Kentucky, Robert M. Fischer, director.*

Percent of Costumes Rented

Percent	Responses
0	49
1 to 25	34
26 to 50	30
51 to 75	3
76 to 100	16

Source If Not Rented

Source (*other than rented*)	*Total Responses*
Made and retained by cast members	35
Made and retained by group	83
Available in costume collection	35
Anywhere they can find them	12

(Some groups reported more than one source)

Whatever the source, plan on having all costumes at least seven to ten days prior to opening night; ten to fourteen days ahead if the costumes are being made locally. Don't

even consider alternate dates. Allow plenty of time for fittings, alterations, improvements, and final approval.

Regardless of how costumes are obtained, they represent a substantial portion of the production budget. Even costumes in storage must be dry-cleaned and spruced up before they are fit to use. Costume expenditures should be approached with care as soon as the cast has been chosen. This allows time for measurements, getting quotes from rental firms, and pricing the yard goods necessary for homemade costumes.

RENTING COSTUMES

Is it better to rent the costumes or to have the group make them locally? The answer depends on personal preference and budget. Some groups don't want to go to the trouble of making their own. Some groups just couldn't manage otherwise. To groups that draw large audiences the costume rental expense isn't as large a percent of their budget. Some groups are willing to pay for the professional touch. Period costumes for such musicals as *The King*

```
MANHATTAN  COSTUME  CO.,  INC.
          RENTALS  AND  MADE  TO  ORDER
614 WEST 51st STREET      •      NEW YORK 19, NEW YORK      •      CIRCLE 7-2396


              THE UNSINKABLE MOLLY BROWN  -  Costume Plot

    Act 1, Scene 1  Exterior  of the Tobin shack, Hannibal, Missouri.  1900

        SHAMUS TOBIN (Father).............Ragged, unkempt attire

        3 TOBIN BROTHERS..................Similar to above

        MOLLY............................Ragged dress with bloomers

        PRIEST...........................Cassock, hat

    Act 1, Scene 2  Exterior of the Saddle Rock Saloon, Leadville, Colorado.
                    Late at night.  Weeks later

        MINERS...........................Assorted rough and dirty shirts, pants, hats, boots.

        JOHNNY BROWN.....................Miner's garb, only more attractive

        PROSTITUTES......................Assorted garrish dresses

    Act 1, Scene 3  Saddle Rock Saloon, night, weeks later

        BURT.............................Miners garb

        CHARLIE MORGAN (owner)...........Shirt, pants, vest, apron

        MINERS...........................Repeat

        MOLLY............................Add mackinaw jacket

        PROSTITUTES......................Repeat

        JOHNNY BROWN.....................Optional change of shirt or add jacket

    Act 1, Scene 4  Exterior of Saddle Rock Saloon, Sunday night, three weeks later

        MINERS...........................Repeat

        TOWNSWOMEN.......................Assorted cotton dresses, bonnets

        CHRISTMAS MORGAN.................Repeat

        MOLLY............................Simple cotton dress

    Act 1, Scene 5  Johnny's log cabin, a month later

        JOHNNY...........................Repeat

        MOLLY............................Repeat

    Act 1, Scene 6  On the road to Johnny's cabin.  Three weeks later

        CHRISTMAS MORGAN.................Add coat and bowler

        TOWNSWOMEN.......................Repeat

    Act 1, Scene 7  Johnny's cabin, a few minutes later.

        MOLLY............................Add apron, camisole, skirt

        CHRISTMAS MORGAN.................Repeat

        JOHNNY...........................Repeat or change shirt

        MINERS...........................Repeat
```

(Figure 8-1—Example of a Costume Plot)

and I, Camelot, Kismet, The Sound of Music, or *Once Upon a Mattress* pose more of a costume problem than *West Side Story, Bells Are Ringing, Bye Bye Birdie,* and are more likely to be rented. Musicals in which most costumes can easily be adapted from regular street clothes are more likely to be completely assembled locally.

The rate for rented costumes averages $10 to $15 per costume. Unique detailed costumes cost more. If the group knows they are going to rent their costumes, a reservation should be placed with the costumer as soon as the show selection has been decided. The costume supply house will then supply a free costume plot and detailed cost estimate for all the costumes listed in the plot. The order isn't placed until measurements are completed months later, but the advance reservation ensures the best available costumes come performance time. And there is no obligation to rent each and every costume listed in the plot.

Free costume plots are available for the asking from any of these major costume suppliers:

Brooks-Van Horn Costumes
16 West 61st Street
New York, N.Y. 10023
or
232 North 11th Street
Philadelphia, Pa. 19107

Manhattan Costume Company
614 West 51st Street
New York, N.Y. 10019

Barnes Costume Company
1304 West Fourth Street
Davenport, Iowa 52802

Eaves Costume Company, Inc.
151 West 46th Street
New York, N.Y. 10036

When requesting costume plots be sure to include the title of the musical and performance dates. With the costume plot the group will receive confirmation of costume availability for the scheduled dates. According to Brooks-Van Horn Costume Co., "the demand for costumes is heaviest between late October and Christmas vacation and again from early February through the end of May." Groups planning musical productions within these periods would do well to get their rental reservations in early to avoid disappointment. During these peak periods it is also wise to allow considerably more than the "minimum 3-week delivery time" quoted by the costume supply house.

The biggest disadvantage in renting costumes is that there's no opportunity to inspect the goods until it is too late. Should some parts or even whole costumes be inadvertently left out of the order, it could create a real problem. Often these problems can be overcome by renting costumes locally.

A quick check in the local Yellow Pages under "Costumes—Masquerade and Theatrical—Rental" or reference to *Simon's Directory of Theatrical Materials, Services, and Information* will reveal nearby sources of costume rental. If the local suppliers don't have the necessary costumes in stock, chances are they will make them up special for your use and future rentals. The more advance notice the costumer is given, the more likely he is to undertake a special set of *new* costumes for your group's use. Of course, the biggest advantage in ordering from a local supplier is the opportunity of seeing the costumes before they are ordered or even selecting materials and supervising the tailoring operation.

WHEN COSTUMES ARE MADE
WITHIN THE GROUP

Making costumes within the group does not save a lot of money, but if they are retained in the group's costume collection for future use there will be certain long-range savings. If it is decided to make the costumes, a qualified designer and/or head seamstress to direct the costume-making operation is necessary. This person should have a good knowledge of yard goods, a fine sense of color, and be a wizard with needle, thread, and sewing machine. He must also be able to adapt or make patterns to fit his designs (and the person playing the role).

The task of costume making may be done entirely by a costume committee. Individuals (usually the chorus only) can be required to make their own with materials provided by the group. Requiring individuals to make their own costumes, however, is, in a way, penalizing them for being in the show. The author would not recommend this procedure or any other that might restrict tryouts by making extra demands on participants. Such practice is a carry-over from old dancing schools. Plus, when uncoordinated individuals make costumes, they may not all turn out the same. Different sewing styles and "personal touches" can make a world of difference.

A costume is nothing more than a costume. It does not need to be constructed like regular street wear. It need only look good from 15 feet away. Linings, for the most part, are not needed. Hems can be basted in quickly. Parts can be pinned together. In short, the finer, time-consuming parts of sewing can be breezed over in a fraction of the time spent in making street apparel. Producing on a mass-production basis, a small group of dedicated people can uniformly costume the whole show in the time it would take to teach twenty people what to do. Some finishing work, such as sewing on sequins, bric-a-brac, and the like, can be farmed out to volunteers.

DESIGNING COSTUMES

Designing costumes is a detailed task that includes a lot more than rendering a creation

WOMENS DEPARTMENT
THIS BLANK FOR FEMALE COSTUMES ONLY

Sheet No._____

BROOKS - VAN HORN Est. 1852 *Theatrical Costumers*

16 WEST 61st STREET   NEW YORK, N. Y. 10023   (212) PLaza 7-5800

Name _____   Address STREET _____

                                                    CITY _____

Organization _____

Title of Production _____

Date of Dress Rehearsal _____ Dates of Play _____ Date to ship _____ How ship _____ Terms _____

Unless credit is established, the terms are one-third cash with order. Balance C. O. D. Plus Ret. Express Charges.

No. of Costumes	NAME OF PERSON	NAME OF CHARACTER	CHEST OR BUST	WAIST	HIP	Waist to Floor	HEIGHT	WEIGHT	HAT	SHOE	NECK TO WAIST (FRONT)	NECK TO WAIST (BACK)	GIRTH

NOTE: Wigs, Footwear or Props are not included unless agreed upon, for which an extra charge is made. If wanted, insert in proper column with size and remarks. Draw tape measure closely around chest and waist, over vest and under coat. Ladies' skirts, full length, waist to floor. Costumes may be altered if not cut. All damages and shortages charged for.

(Figure 8-2)   Costume Order Form

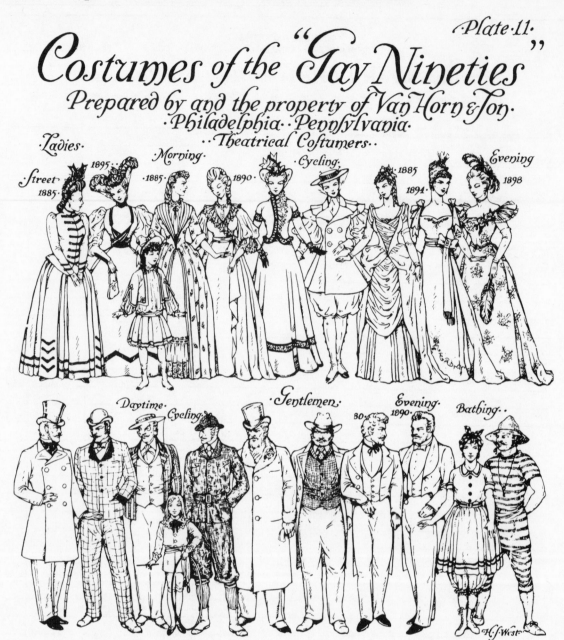

Dress Through the Ages—*one source of researching costume authenticity.*

on a sketch pad. The designer, perhaps with the help of a head seamstress, is responsible for choosing and attaching material swatches to his designs. He must select or create patterns that will enable the head seamstress and members of the costume committee to make the costume. Designs must be prepared in time for early production staff meetings. A talented designer can design around stock items (i.e., leotards, suits, sportswear, previous costumes, etc.) and make creative use of materials that can be purchased in quantity, at substantial savings to the group.

If costumes are to be period pieces, the designer must research the styles of the period. A number of costume plates are available for this purpose. One source is a compact volume entitled *Dress Through the Ages,* available at nominal charge from the Brooks-Van Horn Costume Co. This book contains hundreds of illustrations that will help the designer and director better understand the costume descriptions written in the script.

The head seamstress and the designer could be the same person, but not necessarily. If they are not the same person, the designer must work closely with the head seamstress. The function of the head seamstress is the actual production of the costumes. This usually involves laying out the patterns; supervising several pinning and cutting operations; making sample chorus outfits; close supervision and a personal hand in making principal costumes; and supervising alteration activities. Of course, there are a 1,001 other details involved in costume production, handling, and repair to keep the head seamstress busy. Her job is never really done until the costumes are cleaned and safely in storage weeks after the production is finished. A good head seamstress will also make sure her costumes are exteriorly identified as to show, approximate size, and character of the costume. This information should also be recorded in a central inventory list of available costumes. It is the accurate way to know what is in stock without spending hours hunting through the actual costumes.

Getting together a costume committee to make the large number of costumes required for most musicals is not an easy task. Every group should try to work in a few "interested trainees" each production. Never rely exclusively on a few experienced people. The time will come when they will move on, and without a few people coming up through the ranks, serious delays in the costume operation can result.

Personnel to man the needles, scissors, and sewing machines are comparatively easy to get. The trick is to have the pieces so organized that anyone can do the job. Identical chorus costumes should be assigned to one person along with detailed written instructions and personal supervision on the first assembly. One person makes all the male costumes for a given scene, while another person makes the costumes for the females. And so on down through each chorus scene.

Some sources for costume committee workers are: 1) interested members of the group: Too often people show interest, but aren't given anything concrete to work on. It is difficult to feel involved in a musical unless a person's labors really mean something to the production. Just sewing on buttons doesn't mean much. Button sewers-on frequently get lost after one production (if they stay for one production), but qualified people who rough out costumes or were in complete charge of *all the policemen's costumes,* for example, know that job "couldn't" have been done without them. To them the policemen's costumes will look beautiful on stage. And that person

will be back to make a valuable contribution to the next production; 2) if it's a school group, mothers' clubs are a good prospect (however, watch out for the mother who has a daughter in the chorus); 3) ladies' church societies; 4) home economics teachers and students; 5) sewing circles; and 6) active lady senior citizens groups, retirement villas, activity groups, and the like.

All these groups offer experienced personnel under special circumstances. Cultivation of these sources provides a solution to the head seamstress and a real purpose to the contributors' activities.

OTHER COSTUME SOURCES

The type, style, authenticity, and color of the costumes are a problem to the musical production just as they are a problem to straight plays. The total number of costumes required for a musical is the real rub. To help overcome this problem without running a big costume-rental bill or saving on homemade material cost, check local second-hand stores, the Goodwill, Salvation Army Centers, St. Vincent de Paul shops, and the like. Clothing items found in such outlets provide the ideal *base* for some costumes. Sometimes they are just the ticket "as is" (after cleaning, of course). Often hats, coats, men's suits, women's dresses, etc., can be purchased cheaper than similar items could be made or rented.

The family storeroom or grandma's attic can often produce a cache of 1920's and 1930's fashions. With a little sprucing up, they make ideal costumes for a good many musicals.

Any of these help cut down the total number of costumes needed, even if they're just chorus costumes.

As the number of groups presenting musicals increases, it would be surprising if community theatre organizations and large school districts didn't organize central costume collections of period and special costumes. Another possibility would be a working agreement between production groups whereby a loan policy could be worked out for mutual use of each other's costume collections. An organization might even assemble a set of costumes for a popular musical and rent the complete set to other groups upon the conclusion of their own production.

The large number of costumes required for musical productions represents a sizable portion of the production budget. Any method that reduces costume expenditures, without sacrificing quality or inhibiting the performer who must wear it, can free dollars to use elsewhere in the production.

COSTUME ACCESSORIES

Certain "props" are the responsibility of the costume department. The following table lists the type of props that fall under this responsibility:

Those Worn on the Head: Wigs or other false hairpieces, combs and other hair ornaments, hats, headdresses, veils, caps, earrings, necklaces, and makeup.

Those Worn on the Hands or Arms: Gloves, mitts, mittens, rings, bracelets, and armlets.

Those Carried in the Hand: Fans, snuff boxes, muffs, handkerchiefs, purses and other handbags, umbrellas, canes and walking sticks.

Those Worn on the Feet or Legs: Boots, shoes, spats, stockings, socks, anklets, garters, and sandals.

Those Worn Over a Garment: Shawls, ties and cravats, collars, cuffs, aprons, belts and suspenders.

Those Added Directly to a Garment: Buttons, braids, laces, pockets, bows, ribbons, furs, feathers (usually sewn on).
(Courtesy of Barnes Costume Company)

ANIMAL COSTUMES

One of the highlights in *Can-Can* is all the animals in the Adam and Eve ballet. The New York productions of *Mr. President* (elephant); *Camelot* (jousting horses); *Hello, Dolly!* (trolley horse); and many others used people (usually dancers) in animal costumes. These clever designs added tremendously to the overall effect of the specific number and to the whole show. In the case of the Adam and Eve ballet, animal characters are essential, but in all the other examples the expensive animal costumes were frosting on the cake, the type of thing people expect to see on Broadway. It's fine to have such lavish touches in local productions, but they're the type of item that should come last in budget and preparation. Too often a big push for such costumes takes precedence over more essential items. Never trade an extraneous costume or effect and jeopardize the overall show. They're still nice, but save them until all the basics are taken care of.

Bye Bye Birdie, *Westside High School, Omaha, Nebraska, W. L. Kellogg, director.*

The Amorous Flea, *Memphis State University, Memphis, Tennessee, Chan Cunningham, director.*

The King and I, *Ursuline College, Louisville, Kentucky, Robert M. Fischer, director.*

QUICK CHANGES

There have been some fast changes in plays, but musicals such as *The Sound of Music, Little Me, The Apple Tree, Jennie, Mame,* and *Hello, Dolly!* border on the impossible. (God bless those zippers, every one!) To keep the production from fouling up on a lightning-fast costume change, consider these ideas: 1) A costume changing booth right on stage. Three or four flats roped together work just fine. 2) Underdressing. Nothing new, but worth mentioning. 3) The early exit: At the end of a production number or applause-getting scene, the subject of the quick change exits on the last beat. He might be halfway changed by the time the applause dies down. 4) Doubles.

MAKEUP

Makeup poses no special problems in musical productions, with the possible exception of dancers. The tremendous activities in which dancers engage rule out loose-fitting wigs, makeup that will not withstand heavy perspiration, or any other makeup application that will hinder the dancer's movement.

Special makeup designs may be planned in advance with the use of a makeup plot sheet, but of course nothing is as good as working it out on the person who will wear it.

Professionals are skilled in applying their own makeup. Only in rare cases is a makeup technician employed. Nonprofessionals, however, are not skilled and usually require some supervision. Without it, the makeup procedure is likely to get out of hand. In a very large cast some kind of makeup schedule is almost essential.

Some groups have a professional hair stylist come in and style each principal girl's hair to fit the period or style of the production. It is a nice gesture and adds immeasurably to the girl's morale, at a time when she really needs it. Often prestige hair stylists (with a theatrical glint in their eyes) will perform such a service just for mention or an ad in the program. It is a good way to show off their ability and provides a civic service in which they are particularly valuable.

One last word of caution. Some people are allergic to some makeup. Girls whose systems reject certain makeups are aware of the fact, but unwary males, who might be applying makeup for the first time, could discover some irritating side effects. The author has witnessed some nasty burning skin rashes and one bad case of hives. If at all possible, a makeup rehearsal three weeks or so before opening would flush out any such cases. This avoids performer miseries during the important dress rehearsal or opening performances when such ailments are compounded by many other things.

Buttoning Up

The glamour and splendor basic to most musical theatre productions are often more important in nonprofessional productions than they are in a professional production where magnetic performers can focus the audience's attention. Costuming, and to some extent makeup, are extensions of the all-important settings. They should reflect the proper color and excitement for which they are intended, without overpowering the character or the audience.

Costumes are a major expense. They should be planned for early and obtained by the most economical method possible to achieve the standard decided upon by the productions staff.

CHAPTER IX   Lighting, Sound, and Special Effects

"Dig We Must"

Follow any midtown Manhattan street for a few blocks and you're sure to see three things: pedestrians who haven't the slightest concern for traffic lights, a new skyscraper going up, and a series of diggings protected by barricades stenciled "Dig We Must." The latter are portable monuments to Con Edison, the New York City power and electric company. Whenever a "Dig We Must" barricade sprouts in or near the theatre district it seems that the streets are turned into instant parking lots. For a person driving to the next performance, this can be a cause of more than slight irritation.

Creative stage lighting can also be a cause of bewilderment and despair because the people who are accomplished in this art remain in short supply. But just as the "Dig We Must" signs (and all that goes with them) are an absolute must, so is good dramatic lighting in musical productions.

Professional theatre has progressed from coal-oil and gas lanterns to an era of specialized directional lighting. For anyone who hasn't had the opportunity to see professional lighting, they have merely to venture backstage of a New York musical production to change their whole perspective on lighting technique. The scene is one of thousands of lights. Almost solid lights, each one carefully aimed for a special spot in the production. All colors, all sizes, directed from every possible angle.

Nonprofessional theatre can never hope to match the lighting standards now set for Broadway musicals. Yet too many groups rely completely on general lighting to do the job. Some groups don't even provide enough light to make certain performance areas visible. In a musical each scene should be lit separately to achieve the desired effect. Some lights may be used for only one scene, but usually the circuits can be worked out to allow principal lights to be used for several different settings.

LIGHTING TECHNIQUES

Professionals use many smaller lights to achieve their lighting effects. Most nonprofessional groups will find it more efficient to use fewer larger lights to get approximately the same effects. For example, professionals may use 20 or 30 small spotlights from as many different angles on a given position. Nonprofessionals might use 4 "fresnels" (general spot or area lights) and 2 "lekos" (focusing directional lights) from above and from each side to achieve a similar effect.

Whatever equipment is used, one important principle remains the same in doing musicals that is not necessarily true in plays. That is a system by which the lights on the actors and playing area are different from the lights on the setting. This prevents a lot of moving shadows; adds lighting flexibility in scene changes; allows dimming lights on the set to focus attention on singers; plus better overall illumination of the greater number of people onstage; and so on. General lighting by means of overhead strip lights and/or footlights is a mistake left in the past. It's been years since a Broadway musical used any footlights at all. Overhead striplights and vertical striplights in the wings, however, are still used quite often in conjunction with high-powered directional lighting. Try to light actors and downstage playing areas from in front of the proscenium arch as much as possible, making sure some lighting is low enough to eliminate face shadows.

The follow spot is almost a necessity in professional-like musical production. Two are even better than one. A modern technique in this regard is to use follow spots backstage in forward loft positions. If this is done, it takes at least two follow spots, one on each side. Never use darker-colored gels in a follow spot. The effect is too phony. ·

One could go on for books with other examples of basic lighting—and many people have. Next to costuming, there are probably more books written on sets and lighting than on any other production function. Although most of these books are oriented for straight play production, the principles found in the lighting chapters are also sound for musical

Lighting battens brought in and made part of the set on a large stage to help shrink a proscenium production of The Fantasticks, *directed by Patrick S. Gilvary for the University of Dayton Players, Dayton, Ohio. Orchestra was used onstage behind scrim.*

production. The only trick is to plan enough circuit flexibility in the lighting plan to allow for numerous lighting changes.

What any specific group needs to know about lighting varies tremendously with the size of their stage, the show, and the set. The best thing a lighting designer or technician can know is the lighting capacity of each type of lighting unit. With a firm grasp of this limited knowledge it becomes fairly easy to plan the lighting moods requested by the director and to determine in advance the amount of lighting equipment necessary to do the show.

The single most useful tool that the author has found in this respect is a catalog entitled *Century Theatre Lighting.* Copies may be obtained from Century Lighting, Inc., 3 Entin Road, Clifton, N.J. 07014.

SOUND

Sound effects serve major functions in many musicals. Care should be taken to maintain a balance of sound level between sound effects and the orchestra. Also, try to place the source of sound as close to the orchestra as practical.

The orchestra itself can be the source of

"live" sound effects. Besides musical instruments, a parade of sound-producing devices exist that can be used to accent a musical or dance number or used as a sound effect during the dialogue. *West Side Story* is probably the best example of using the orchestra as a source of sound effects. The original show incorporated two percussionists, one to play the drums and one to operate all the sound effects.

Unfortunately, many scores that have used orchestral sound are not so noted on the manuscript available to local groups. The local production staff should be on the alert for places in the score where such sound effects would add flavoring. A close hearing of the original cast album with this in mind can also be very enlightening. If there is a question as to the types of orchestral sound devices available, see your musical director.

Recorded sound effects are available through any theatrical supply house and sometimes through the leasing agent for the specific musical you are doing. In addition to these traditional suppliers, you might check your local record shop. Hi-fi bugs have been demanding all sorts of odd noise and sound effects to show off their latest home entertainment rigs.

Audio Fidelity, Inc., for example, has a series of more than twenty 33⅓ LP sound-effect albums with flawless sounds, which often cost less than sounds especially prepared for theatrical use.

SPECIAL EFFECTS

When Hinesie throws a knife in *The Pajama Game,* when a pot of gold sprouts a rainbow in *Finian's Rainbow,* when smoke clogs the pub in *Oliver!,* or when *Peter Pan* takes to the air, you are in the area of special effects. This holds true too for the fog in *Baker Street,* the rain in *110 in the Shade,* magical effects in *Carnival,* snowfall in *Little Mary Sunshine,* and the movie in *Fiorello!* Flash appearances, trap doors, an illusion set, and other special effects make a list that goes on forever. They are as many and varied as authors and producers have been able to make them. However, not too many of them are really new.

The main reason for mentioning them here is to focus attention on a factor that is often faked in nonprofessional musical production. When this happens it's for one of two reasons. Either the special effect wasn't planned well enough in advance, or it was decided at the

Theatrical lighting and good special effects help convey the atmosphere of Oliver! *Jack Nakano directed this staging of the musical for Youth Theatre Productions, Santa Barbara, California.*

TIM PUTZ PHOTOGRAPHY

Lighting plays an important part throughout Brigadoon. In this production, directed by William Y. Hardy for the Hill Country Arts Foundation, Ingram, Texas, the bridge and mysterious land appeared and disappeared with the help of lighting and scrim.

Tight area lighting was used for this scene played on a wagon near downstage wing in front of a flown-in insert panel. Patrick S. Gilvary directed the University of Dayton Players, Dayton, Ohio, in this production of Wonderful Town.

outset not to go to the extra trouble. In the first case it could be disastrous for certain shows such as *High Spirits, Carnival, Peter Pan*—and what would *Goldilocks, Finian's Rainbow,* or *110 in the Shade* be without their final miracles? Advance planning for special effects is a must in building sets to accommodate spring knives for *The Pajama Game.* "Hernando's Hideaway" from the same show could also go astray if ample rehearsal isn't devoted to match lighting techniques.

For the groups that think certain special effects are beyond their capacity there can be only one word of advice: At least try it before you give up. Special effects make the show more professional. In many cases they are actually *part* of the show. Preplanning and a little ingenuity can work wonders. If problems do develop, contact the leasing agent or a theatrical supply house. Be sure to mention that you need the most economical means (or whatever your budget allows) to accomplish the effect. They will usually outline various procedures in the interest of keeping you as a good client.

Again, it is well to mention that many excellent books are available on the subject of lighting, sound, and special effects. Should the production-staff members have problems in these areas it would be advisable to consult one of these specific publications.

(*Figure 9-1*)

Flying in Peter Pan, Superman, *or* High Spirits *is great fun and high professionalism. In the case of* Peter Pan, *four lines are required. For greatest flexibility, these are hung center stage, 2' to 4' apart on a perpendicular line to the proscenium arch. The flyers can then travel in any direction and land at any given spot simply by standing, in rehearsal, on the spot where they want to land, flying and marking their landing spot. When they fly from this mark, they will end up at their precise destination.*

The aerial rigging for this system, as designed by student Richard Davies for Beaverton High School, is almost as simple. In addition to the notes on the diagram, these points are important: There must be at least 10' of empty fly space both up- and downstage (no lights, battens, etc.). Sandbags used for counterweights should be approximately one-half the weight of the character using that line the most. This permits easy flying as well as allowing the actor to walk freely with the line attached. The system is operated by pulling back on the rear of the loops to fly, pulling the front of the loops to land and walk. The front of the loops are tied off when not in use.

This flying system is safe, but fragile. All wires must be checked before every show. Any kinks, nicks, tangles, etc., render the wires unsafe.

Each flyer wears a flying harness under his costume. These harnesses are usually rented.

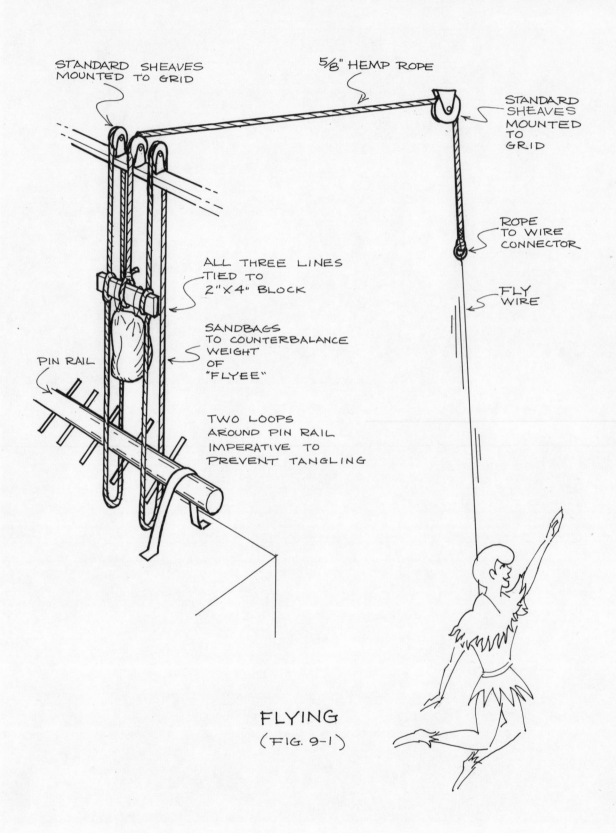

STANDARD SHEAVES
MOUNTED TO GRID

5/8" HEMP ROPE

STANDARD
SHEAVES
MOUNTED
TO
GRID

ALL THREE LINES
TIED TO
2"X4" BLOCK

ROPE
TO WIRE
CONNECTOR

FLY
WIRE

SANDBAGS
TO COUNTERBALANCE
WEIGHT
OF
"FLYEE"

PIN RAIL

TWO LOOPS
AROUND PIN RAIL
IMPERATIVE TO
PREVENT TANGLING

FLYING

(FIG. 9-1)

The Fantasticks *at Aloha High School, Beaverton, Oregon, directed by Robert R.* Buseick.

CHAPTER X Budget, Tickets, Program, and Promotion

"Dollars and Sense"

There are two types of people in the professional theatre, the creative people and the money people. There are no thin lines separating them. The producers might spend money *tastefully,* but their chief concern is *money.* In fact, it is almost always somebody else's money. The traditional arrangement is for the backers to put up 100 percent of the money for a 50 percent interest in the show. The money coming in from ticket sales is divided as follows: The theatre takes about 30 percent of the gross income off the top, then salaries and production expenses are paid, after which the producer usually receives 1 percent of the gross until the investors are paid back their original investment and as much as 40 or 50 percent thereafter. The only liability of a producer, who acts as the general partner in a limited partnership (as is nearly always the case) is when he exceeds his production budget and the show flops. Then he is stuck for all production and closing expenses in excess of the backer's investment.

Although financing methods for nonprofessional productions differ widely from the Broadway setup, the problem still remains that creative people usually aren't good money people. Yet too often the nonprofessional producer-director is also required to supervise the money handling. Theatrical productions are a business and must be conducted as such, and whereas money handling and theatrical creativity are often in direct opposition to each other, both are a *must* to every successful musical production.

During the course of some nonprofessional musical productions, as much as $20,000 might change hands. With several thousand dollars involved, a sound, cut-and-dried money-handling procedure is essential. It should be simple and foolproof. No one system will fit every group's needs, but the following setup is one proven method that can be used as it is or adapted to individual group needs.

THE BUDGET

There are two elements of a theatrical financing operation: the money going out for production expenses and the money coming in from ticket sales. It is recommended that these two elements be kept completely separate if at all possible. (This means sufficient money to cover preproduction expenses, such as good faith deposits, cash purchases, etc., must be available in the bank.) Two bank accounts should be set up: one to draw on for production expenses and one in which to deposit ticket sales money. Deposits from ticket sales should be made daily, retaining only enough cash for adequate change. Withdrawal of production expense funds should be made by the producer-director or the business manager. Sometimes a petty cash fund will be necessary.

So much for the money. Now for the real problem: how to account for it. The basic rule is to get a receipt for every expenditure. If the person making the expenditure fails to get a receipt, notation regarding the amount and purpose of the expenditure should be made on a 3 x 5 card or similar scrap of paper.

Receipts are then filed in a series of 9 x 12 envelopes. On the face of the envelope is duplicated a standard form to record each transaction.

Make budget envelopes for each production function, listing the amount budgeted for each category:

Royalties and Material Rental Fees
Costumes
Scenery
Salaries (if any)
Properties
Lighting and Special Effects
Publicity and Promotion
Programs
Miscellaneous (theatre rental, concessions, etc.)

153

BUDGET ENVELOPE

SHOW _My Fair Lady_   DATES _Feb. 14-15-16 and 21-22-23_

PRODUCTION DEPARTMENT _Costumes_   ENVELOPE # _7_

BUDGET $ _750_

EXPENDITURE(Purchases, rentals,shipping, etc.)	COST	COST ACCUMULATIVE	RECEIPT
Rental Costumes	$425.00	$425.00	send check
Henry's Hat	11.44	436.44	cash register
Feathers and plumes	24.95	461.39	receipt enclosed
Yard goods	73.50	534.89	charged
Zippers, thread, etc	5.35	540.24	receipt enclosed
Shawl	8.00	548.24	receipt enclosed
Dry-clean servant uniforms	13.50	561.74	receipt enclosed
Coats and suits from Second-Hand Store	63.80	625.54	cash receipt encl.

TOTAL SPENT $_____

(Figure 10-1)
Cover of Budget Envelope

TICKET CONTROL ENVELOPE

Show-_____ Production Dates_____

TICKET PRICES: Season_____ Adult____ Student____

DATE	STARTING CHANGE	ADULT #SOLD	ADULT $SOLD	STUDENT # SOLD	STUDENT $ SOLD	TOTAL #	TOTAL $	BANK DEPOSIT	ENDING CHANGE

Ticket Sales Summary

DATE OF PERF.	SEASON TICKETS	ADULT ADMISSIONS	STUDENT ADMISSIONS	TOTAL	$ VALUE

(*Figure 10-2*)
Cover of Ticket Accounting Envelope

As receipts or notations of expenditures are obtained, they should be recorded on the face of the proper envelope and inserted therein. Thus, each expenditure is quickly disposed of, and it is easy to detect expenditures that are exceeding the budget amount. The final accounting is prepared as each receipt is recorded. There is no financial chaos after the show closes. That "where-did-all-the-money-go" feeling is avoided, and the detailed accounting is valuable for budgeting the next musical production. Under no circumstances should cash be kept in any accounting envelopes.

Certain amounts to be budgeted will be known in advance. (Royalty and material rental fees, costume rental, theatre rental, etc.) Others will need to be estimated. If the group is seeking financial success, it is wise to keep total production expense budgets within 65 percent of potential gross ticket sales. A lesser percent should be used if attendance is traditionally under 75 percent capacity, or if the auditorium seats more than 1,000 people.

Accounting for the box-office operation is a bit more difficult. A special 9 x 12 envelope is required. If reserved seats are being offered, the box-office staff will also need a seating chart for each performance.

The special ticket accounting envelope should allow enough entry spaces to cover the ticket-selling season. If the group is selling season tickets, the ticket accounting envelopes should be ready for the full slate of productions and properly marked as season tickets are disbursed. Since most season-ticket prices are at a reduced rate, this accounting should be separate. Reserve seating charts should be marked in a contrasting color of ink.

TICKETS

Admission prices vary from 50¢ student tickets to as much as $5 or more when a name professional appears with a nonprofessional group in a lead role. Most ticket prices, however, are in the $1.25-to-$2.50 range. If there is any doubt about what to charge, you might try the following pattern: Put a price on what you think your show is worth to the audience. Reduce the price about 20 to 25 percent for advance sale. If advance sales don't amount to about 15 percent capacity (about 12 percent for auditoriums seating more than the 1,000) then it's a good bet that people are staying away because the price is too high. (Not valid for groups who have a reputation for doing under-par shows.)

Every theatrical production runs into the problem of ticket printing, handling, selling,

and accounting. In the interest of a complete production guide, the following ideas are submitted for the readers' evaluation.

Plain tickets can be produced on an office duplicating machine or fancy Broadway-style tickets can be ordered from a number of firms. The deciding factor on the type of tickets may be the method by which they are offered to the public. General admission tickets can be professionally printed locally for about $15 or $20. A different color "stock" (paper or cardboard) should be used for each night, but the printing remains the same. All production dates appear on each ticket, and the proper date is circled to correspond to the color of the ticket. If tickets are being given away (as is often the case in city recreation and industrial productions), the office duplicating machine is plenty good enough. Duplicate on different color stock as previously mentioned for general admission tickets.

It is the author's conviction that it is better to sell tickets to a musical production on a reserved-seat basis. A professional type of ticket costs from $20 to $200, depending on the size of each theatre and the number of performances for which tickets will be required.

A less expensive way to achieve the same goal, also a little less fancy, is to have a special regulation-size ticket printed for each night omitting section and seat location. These are printed in by hand with an appropriate marking pencil. It's a time-consuming job, but it constitutes considerable dollar savings over the individually numbered tickets printed by the professional supplier.

Sometimes the printing of tickets is sponsored by a local merchant. Restaurants, airlines, nightclubs, banks, savings and loan companies, etc., are often interested in having their ad appear on the reverse side of the tickets or on a small ticket envelope. The cost of such an ad can substantially or entirely cover the cost of printing tickets and envelopes. Firms sponsoring ticket printing should also be acknowledged in the program.

THE BOX OFFICE

The handling of tickets is a thankless and tedious job, but it, just like every other function, is a vital part of show biz. Haphazard box-office operation has plagued just about every group at one time or another.

People who will gladly undertake box-office supervision are hard to find. People who are good at the job are rare. There probably never has been a person who joined a theatrical group

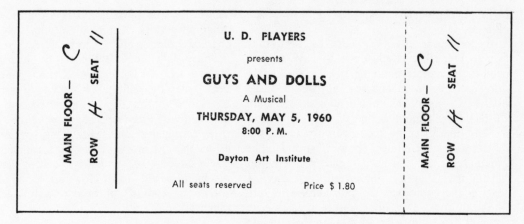

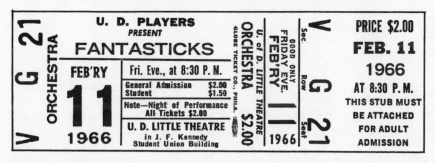

Evolution of reserved-seat tickets at the University of Dayton. The Guys and Dolls *ticket was school-printed and seat locations were filled in by hand. For* Damn Yankees *a more professional-looking ticket was prepared by a local printer but still filled in. For* Little Mary Sunshine *professional tickets were printed, but "student" was rubber-stamped on the back for reduced price admission. Hand work was completely eliminated for* The Fantasticks *by using an adult admission stub. This, of course, was removed on student sales.*

for the sole purpose of working in the box office.

As inhumane as it may seem, the best solution to box-office efficiency is to have as few people as possible handling tickets, preferably only one person in charge and two or three assistants, depending on the number of hours the box office remains open.

This doesn't mean that everyone can't sell tickets to a reserved-seat show. Cast and other group members can sell numbered coupon tickets that may be exchanged for reserved seats at the box office. Coupon holders merely phone the box office upon purchase to reserve the best available seats. In making their phone reservations they give the number on their coupon, which tells the box-office manager who sold the ticket and where to collect the money. Such coupons must be clearly marked *"Phone Reservation Required," "Must be Redeemed for Reserved Seat in Advance,"* or some other such imprint to make sure popular performances won't be oversold or that advance ticket customers won't be disappointed.

No show, musical or otherwise, has ever suffered from a good advance sale. Two popular advance-sale methods are the season ticket and the theatre party. These methods will probably be most useful to university and little-theatre groups.

There are many ramifications of the season ticket. Usually tickets to three or more shows are sold as a group prior to the season opening—the same seats for each show. Some discount is provided as an incentive for immediate purchase, usually enough so that admission to one show is free. From limited experience it seems that having at least one musical in a slate of theatrical productions boosts season-ticket sales. (A successful musical also seems to swell nonseason ticket attendance at straight play productions.) Season tickets require a special promotion campaign, but it is usually worth the effort.

A theatre party provides a per-ticket discount to large group purchasers, or tickets are sold to an outside group or organization at the regular box-office price and said groups get a "donation" on top of the regular ticket price. The latter theatre-party method is virtually useless for nonprofessional productions, but if a given group has enjoyed a string of successful productions and ticket demand is high, it may be well worth a try.

Selling Tickets for Dress Rehearsal

Photos should never be taken during a scheduled performance. Both flashbulbs and jack-in-the-box photographers are annoying to other spectators. Yet some groups feel these cherished photos are not to be denied. Another problem is giving all the family members a chance to see the show. Some groups kill both birds by selling "passes" to a dress rehearsal. Photo-taking is permitted and ticket prices are reduced, perhaps to ½ or ¾ the price of regular admission. This practice also offers the cast a chance to perform before an audience and get a better feel of how the production will run. However, the practice should be avoided if there is only one dress rehearsal.

The Program

Years ago a theatrical program was printed for each performance. It was a long sheet resembling a narrow scroll. Its function was chiefly to identify the players of the evening.

Today, a theatrical program must contain the following:

1) Title and author of the show
2) Permission line from the leasing agent
3) Names of the director, choreographer, and musical director
4) Character and cast names
5) Synopsis of scenes
6) Musical numbers
7) Other production staff names
8) Acknowledgments

Normally, this information appears in a small four-page giveaway program that is presented to patrons as they are ushered to their seat. Sometimes this giveaway program contains ads. Some groups even count on profit from program ads to cover production losses. Whatever the purpose, any group who goes to all the trouble of selling ads and running down all the uncollectables certainly deserves everything they get out of it. Just remember one point when the group is obtaining ads: They are not selling advertising, they are collecting donations. The notice that appears in the program has very little, if any, advertising value. So don't get mad if the local supermarket doesn't buy that page ad that is "going to bring them all that business"—because it isn't. Most businesses are besieged by high-school senior annual ads, fraternal organizations, and the like, for this contribution type of advertising, which can only prove them supporters of community activities.

Since the primary function of any group producing a musical show is not selling ads, and since such ads are not required to underwrite the production expenses of a truly suc-

BOB MIDDLESTETTER

Souvenir programs offer the crowning touch to a musical production. While custom-designed program covers can be effective, you can't go wrong with a show's original graphics. Six of the above designs are adapted from the originals. For those who don't immediately recognize them, they are: Oklahoma!, Fanny, My Fair Lady, Redhead, Flower Drum Song, *and* How to Succeed in Business Without Really Trying.

cessful musical, attention can be focused on turning the program into part of the theatre-going experience. Such ideals can be realized in a souvenir program. Instead of putting people to work selling program ads, channel their efforts into providing a souvenir program.

A souvenir program should include all the information included in the giveaway program, plus the following:

1) Production photos, actual scenes with costumes and sets.
2) Photos and write-ups about the director, choreographer, and musical director. (Also, other production people if it is felt necessary.)
3) Photos of the principal players and short biography on each.
4) Photos and biographies of the authors (if available).
5) Production story on why the show was selected, Broadway history, and the group's experience in producing the show.
6) Brief story of the musical.
7) An attractive cover (adapt design from original-cast record jacket or production material).

Only eighteen of the groups surveyed by the Musical Comedy Production Questionnaire mentioned that they published a souvenir program. Two of these groups gave these programs away or had its cost built into the price of the tickets. The latter seems a good method to add prestige to the production without asking the patrons to spend more money upon entering the theatre; particularly in high-school and college productions where dating is common. The boy almost looks cheap if he doesn't shell out for programs.

To print an eight-page souvenir program with a two-color cover (black and a second color) with several photographs costs around $250 for 2,000 copies. (A good creative advertising man can do wonders with one color and maybe a colored paper.) These costs are over and above any fees for photographs or art work.

There are several advantages to having a souvenir program:

1) If sold, a souvenir program could be an extra source of income. Bear in mind, however, you would need to sell 1,000 copies at 25¢ or 500 copies at 50¢ to break even on the average printing cost of $250. A single-sheet giveaway program would still be required.
2) Any group that publishes a good souvenir program adds tremendously to the prestige of their group. It allows the group to give information about the musical that makes the show more interesting to the audience. It gives them something absorbing to read prior to curtain time and something to show to friends when speaking about the performance. And sometimes most important of all, it will be kept for several months or even years before it is discarded. Others will see it and learn about the producing group. Hence, the program itself becomes a long-running ad building favorable or unfavorable impressions. Publish a good souvenir program and you make a good impression on future ticket buyers.
3) If the souvenir program is given away, all the better. This requires only one program. The regular giveaway program normally costs about $40 to $100, depending on the quantity. Since these programs won't be required, the money can be put toward the cost of preparing a souvenir program. If enough money can't be budgeted to cover the entire cost, perhaps one page of ads could be sold to raise the necessary funds. The added value of presenting each member of the audience a comprehensive souvenir program is something that really can't be measured, but to some it could be worth the price of admission.

There is usually a literary person in every group that would be interested in preparing a souvenir program. It is a major accomplishment and a source of great self-satisfaction for the right person. It would be a tedious and time-consuming job for the wrong one. An inexperienced but interested person can do the job easily in about twenty hours, spread out

(Figure 10-5)

Composite layout for an eight-page souvenir program: 1—cover. Page 2—(left column) billing, acknowledgments, (right column) Cast, synopsis of scenes, musical numbers, (orchestra goes here or on page 7). Page 3—photos and write-ups on the principal characters (group bust photo saves photography cost). Page 4—production photos. Page 5—production photos. Page 6—photos and write-ups on the director,

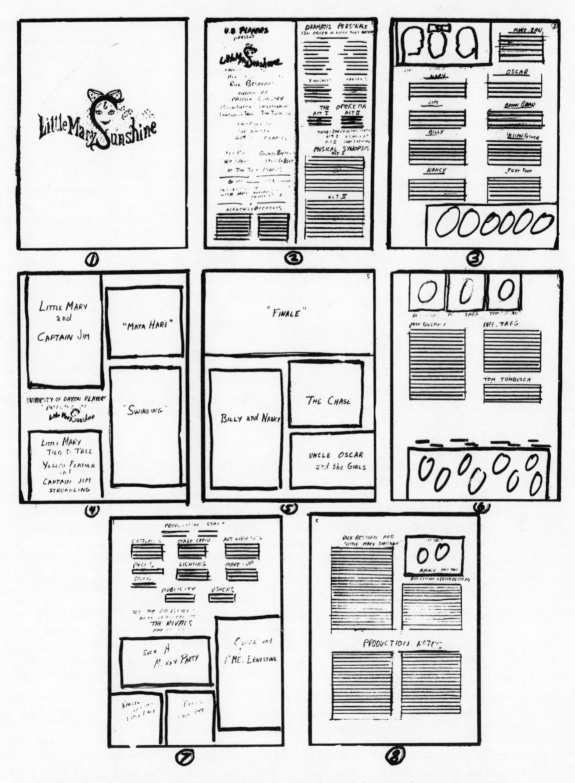

choreographer, and musical director, plus group photo of key members of the production staff (good arty photo of each with his or her tools, etc.). Page 7—names of complete production staff, announcement of future shows, orchestra and/or production photos. Page 8—photo of authors and/or original Broadway star (if available) and write-up on the show's history or plot . . . and production notes on the producing group's own experiences in preparing the production.

over the production. With two or three people to help, the job can be done in seven to ten hours.

An organized procedure is required to make sure everything is included in the souvenir program. One proven method is as follows:

1) Make a layout and/or "printer's dummy." Get prices from two or three printers and make advance arrangements with the one you want.
2) Make up a biography information sheet to be completed by featured cast and production staff members.
3) Type all known copy, i.e., musical numbers, synopsis of scenes, cast of characters, etc.
4) Write biographies from bio-information forms.
5) Design and prepare the cover art (or have an artist do it).
6) Take cast and production staff photos (usually as they appear in dress street clothes).
7) Research the authors and original production information (available for many musicals from Package Publicity Service, Inc., 1564 Broadway, New York, N.Y. 10036).
8) Get final corrected lists of acknowledgments, production crews, etc., and write the production "notes" and the author's biography.
9) Take the production photos at the first dress rehearsal.
10) Get the final information to the printer at least three days prior to opening night. Previous arrangements will need to be made for this type of service. The printer will probably want any available copy a week or two in advance of the last-minute rush material in order to provide a top-quality job and to schedule his work properly.

Besides giving the audience a first-class guide to the production, the souvenir program provides each cast and group member a ready-made production scrapbook for lifelong remembrance. Leftover copies can be given to new group members to show them the type of productions in which they can expect to participate.

A souvenir program may be prepared for either play or musical, but here again, the larger acceptance of the musical makes the job far more practical.

PROMOTION

Regardless of the heavy competition for entertainment time and dollars, people in all walks of life want, and support, the legitimate theatre. Amateur groups have been doing plays for years, and millions of people have enjoyed their own local brand of this theatrical form. Within the single dimension of the play, many people have developed mental blocks as to the type of entertainment they think can be obtained at the local level—and certainly what could be expected from local high schools. The advent of the musical has changed many things. Productions are achieving heights no one ever thought possible, mainly because musicals have more than one dimension. Singing, dancing, music, and the faster pace projected in most book musicals creates an exciting entertainment medium that has never been equaled in any play, variety show, or revue.

Once a group enjoys a truly successful musical production, it is no trick to woo a large percentage of their audience back the next year. The real problem is to get new people to attend for the first time. There are a number of ways to do this, but the best way is a device that show business itself must have created: publicity.

YOU GOTTA LET 'EM KNOW YOU'RE THERE

Publicity is obtained through press releases, interviews, appearances, and a host of other means, limited only by the imagination of the publicity director. The most basic form is the press release. Sometimes this step is passed over because it is considered too much work, but by doing so producers belittle their production effort in the eyes of the public. The public is not formally invited. Without this invitation the public is likely to consider the show an "inside" event, even if they learn about it in some other way (other than advertising).

A publicity release is easy to write and its publication can't do anything but help the current production, as well as the overall reputation of the group mentioned.

WRITING THE PRESS RELEASE

Anyone can write a press release, making sure it includes the pertinent facts: who, what, when, where, the price of tickets, and how they may be obtained. Background on the show, the hit songs it includes, and other sidelights that make interesting copy should be included after the more important facts. The publicity release should also be written as concisely as possible, giving factual data only.

SAMPLE PRESS RELEASE

Released By:
  University of Dayton Players
  300 College Park Avenue
  Dayton, Ohio 45401
  461-5500 Ext. 281

For Release:
  Sunday 2/17/68
  or thereafter

U.D. PLAYERS TO PRESENT THE FANTASTICKS

The University of Dayton Players (who) will present The Fantasticks (what) April 5-6-7 and 19-20-21 (when) at the Boll Theatre located in the J. F. Kennedy Student Union building (where). Tickets are now on sale at the ticket office or by calling 461-5500 Ext. 281 (how).

The show will be directed by Professor Patrick S. Gilvary. The choreographer will be Tom Tumbusch, and Lawrence E. Tagg will serve as musical director. In making the announcement of the production, Gilvary said, "the original production of The Fantasticks was staged in-the-round. Our first problem is to translate the script to our proscenium stage; our second problem will be to choose a cast of only seven actors from the 75 to 100 we expect to try out."

The Fantasticks, with songs by Tom Jones and book and lyrics by Harvey Schmidt, became the longest running off-Broadway play or musical August 4, 1966, when it surpassed the 2,611 performance record previously held by The Threepenny Opera. It opened at the Sullivan Street Playhouse May 3, 1960 and has since played in over 25 foreign countries.

The big song hit of the show is "Try To Remember," but other songs, such as "Soon It's Gonna Rain," have been recorded by several top artists.

The musical was suggested by a play called Les Romanesques by

Edmond Rostand. It deals with two crafty fathers who believe they have the formula for raising teenage children: to get them to do what you want, you tell them they can't. The son and daughter perform true to the theory until they are forced to put up with the stark realities of true love.

The Fantasticks is noted for its charm, tender songs, beautiful language, and flashes of uproarious comedy.

Usually more than one press release is desirable. Presenting a musical offers many unusual opportunities to bring the vital facts before the public. Here is a list of subjects on which separate releases may be made:

1) The selection of show and the dates on which it is to be presented: a general release as illustrated on page 163.
2) Tryouts: A public announcement for people to come and try out for parts.
3) Casting: When casting has been completed, an announcement of the names of the people who won the principal roles is always in order; it is also a good time to give credit to key people on the production staff.
4) Costumes: If the show uses special period or unusual costumes, this always makes a good picture story; costumes of the 1920's always get a good "remember-when" type of story.
5) Rehearsal: Lets the public in for a "private" backstage glimpse of things to come—a good chance to show off some pretty faces.
6) The availability of tickets: If a public box office is being used, the newspaper will usually run a few lines on the opening of the box office.
7) Critics: Good or bad reviews, the critics are publicity. It is customary to invite them by personal letter and to enclose two free tickets, preferably on the aisle about 8 to 10 rows back. A press kit with background information is sometimes provided.
8) Others: Special anniversary shows, the excitement of opening night, children playing an important role, the scholarship the show's profits will provide, or a hundred other ideas, all offer a chance to get the name of the show before the people.

The more publicity circulated and published, the more important the event becomes. Consequently more people will want to see the show. If they come and enjoy themselves, they are a strong potential for future shows. If they don't enjoy themselves, the publicity effort must be even better the next year. There is no publicity like a good production.

Once written, a press release is easy to reproduce. Any method will do as long as it is neat and easy to read. There is no need to type it individually. Representatives of public communications media are accustomed to receiving material in this fashion. Their only concern is news that will be interesting to their readers or listeners. Trying to make them fancy is a waste of time and effort. Make press releases to:

1) Daily newspapers
   a) theatre or amusement sections
   b) arts sections
   c) women's editions
   d) what's-going-on-around-town section
2) Weekly newspapers
3) Suburban newspapers
4) Union newspapers
5) Area armed forces publications
6) Appropriate church bulletins
7) Other theatre groups; high schools, colleges, and community theatres
8) Civic organizations
9) Chamber of Commerce publicity departments
10) Radio stations, AM and FM
11) TV stations
    a) conversation programs
    b) special public-service programs
    c) women's programs
12) Alumni publications
13) Industry publications
14) Library bulletin boards

Publicity kits (consisting of press releases and other background materials) are commercially available. If used, take extra care to tailor the material to local interest. Make sure to mention the director, choreographer, musical director, and the names of principal characters.

Similar information is available from record jackets, script material, or the public library, by author and title. The *Playbill* from the Broadway production is usually available from Playbill, Incorporated, 579 Fifth Avenue, New York, N.Y. 10017, for 35¢ to $5 per copy, depending on the age of the show.

ADVERTISING

Advertising a musical production is not like putting a classified ad in the newspapers. Classified ads can often achieve their purpose in one day. They have one specific goal: to sell a car, hire a secretary, or rent a room. Filling a theatre by means of advertising requires an ad campaign of several weeks, not just a one-time deal. The only exception might be a small town weekly newspaper that all the local people read faithfully for its homespun information and gossip value. But for the most part, stick to publicity and the following economical advertising-promotional activities.

The most traditional means of theatrical advertising is the display card or poster. The poster dates back to days when it was about the only means of advertising. Back then it served to inform the local community that the show was coming to town and tried to arouse interest by trading on the excitement surrounding the magical theatrical undertakings of the time. Early posters exhibited much more copy than is used today, but its purpose remains essentially the same: to inform and interest in a clear and simple way. Too often today these qualities are sacrificed for the sake of "getting attention." If a person must stop to figure out what is being displayed, a poster is not doing the job. Its job is to inform and interest in the time it takes to pass it by. If it can't, it isn't worth the time and money to produce.

To inform, the poster must list the names of the producing group, the title of the production (usually the author's name(s) is included), the place the production is to be presented, the dates of production, and admission prices. Type styles and size can vary, but all important copy material should be readable at a distance of ten feet.

To interest, a poster must graphically illustrate the mood, period, action, style, or theme of the musical in such a way that it is easily communicated to the viewer. The standard size in which this is best achieved is 14″ x 22″ poster board used in the vertical position. These have been the standards in professional theatre for more than 35 years. Larger posters are more difficult to handle, more difficult to place, and make it more difficult for the human eye to grasp the important facts on passing, mainly because the information is unwisely spread out.

A professional-looking poster adds class to a production. An amateurish poster so labels the production. Posters can be improved in content, as well as in method of reproduction.

The illustration subject of the poster makes or breaks the content of any poster. This is often assigned to an artist someone knows or who is a leader in his art class. By assigning the job, you are stuck with about anything he turns out. Frequently such artists know nothing of the show, or just produce a talented (or very untalented) "work of art" void of any value as a poster. (And one artist never tells another artist that his work is lousy.)

There is one sure way to avoid such unhappy situations and improve posters at the same time: Simply adapt the design associated with the original Broadway production. This design has already been exposed in national advertising, on record-album jackets, sheet music, and scores of other media. The design is easy to pick up from any of the previously named items or the rented production materials, by means of photostat, tracing paper, or artistic talent.

Posters can be hand painted or reproduced by silk screening, regular printing, or hand lithographing. Printing is expensive, hand lithographing requires skill, and silk screening is very messy. Hand painting posters is impractical if any quantity is involved. The most universally used method is silk screening. The results can be very professional without much skill. The process involves cutting a stencil from line artwork (or photostat, record jacket, etc.), using a special stencil film. It is then affixed to a silk screen mounted on a printing frame. A separate stencil is required for each color. Two or three colors do a great job. The silk screen and frame cost about $10 or $15. One hundred to 150 posters can be produced for about $15.

PLACING POSTERS

Most merchants will cooperate in placing theatrical posters in a reasonably high traffic location. Store windows, near cash registers, library bulletin boards, shopping centers,

BILL PATTERSON

BOB MIDDLESTETTER

Three posters created and produced by the University of Dayton (a). Although designs for The Boy Friend *and* Guys and Dolls *are artistic, the one for* Little Mary Sunshine *makes the best poster. Besides being adapted from the original design for the show, it is easy to catch all the necessary information at a glance. Imprinted professional posters as in (b) are available from Package Publicity Service.*

church lobbies, schools, community centers, bus terminals, drive-in restaurants, taverns, etc. are excellent locations. Sometimes it is better to call ahead and make arrangements, but usually an armload of posters and a quick OK on the spot gets a greater number of posters placed in a shorter time.

PAINTED SIGNS

Painted outdoor signs are very impressive and very theatrical. An elaborate painted sign in a high traffic location, such as the heart of the business district or along a main thoroughfare, can make many advertising impressions. If the opportunity for such signs is present, by all means meet it with a good display. Again, consider the original Broadway design as its subject.

The main point to keep in mind is where they fit in the promotion strategy. Publicity and small posters should always come first. They are more important because they get the message to a lot more people. The use of a few large outdoor signs in lieu of an aggressive publicity program and 50 to 100 well placed posters has obvious shortcomings. The impact life of a painted outdoor sign is also much shorter, and care must be taken not to erect them too far in advance of opening night. It will be noticed on the first few passes, but once established in the minds of the passersby, will usually go unnoticed. On the other hand, a new publicity article and a small poster in each new location makes a new impression and reminds the viewer of the event.

Some professional outdoor sign companies allow a certain amount of space (perhaps 6 to 12 billboards a year) for use as public service. If your show is marking a special anniversary or other special occasion, mention could be made to the bill-posting company to determine if free space could be provided. This would add tremendous prestige value and if obtained, a special press release should be made—first as publicity for your show, second as proper recognition for the outdoor advertising company.

Painted outdoor signs take a lot of time. They are worthwhile only when they don't jeopardize the musical production or more important publicity and promotion efforts.

LOBBY DISPLAYS

A lobby display near the box office or near the theatre entrance is always a good practice, if only to let people know they are in the right place when they come to buy tickets. Production photos of dress rehearsal mounted on a large board serve the purpose well. Large blowups of good newspaper reviews, individual photos of the leading characters and/or directors, and decorations in the motif of the production also help to generate interest and ticket sales.

Large, single blowup photos of flashy production numbers and/or elaborate settings convey the professionalism of your production better than all the words in the dictionary. One company that specializes in these large photos for Hollywood and Broadway is Foto-Krafters, Inc., 132–134 East Jackson Street, Shelbyville, Indiana. This firm, or any of the other firms specializing in this type of work, will gladly send their price list on request. Most groups find that this extra touch costs far less than they imagine.

FLYERS AND HANDOUTS

Another traditional promotion piece of the professional theatre is the "herald" or flyer. These are small handbills usually about 5½″ x 8½″ in size. They are found in programs, restaurant counters, hotel lobbies, airports, etc. As used by professionals, they are of little value in local promotion. But locally these small posters have value when placed under windshield wipers, hung on college campus bulletin boards, passed out in libraries, mailed to high schools, used in locations where posters are too large, stuffed with department store or bank statements, or otherwise circulated near the time of production. Be sure heralds or flyers have a convenient order coupon at the bottom or on the reverse side for easy ticket ordering.

The best means of producing this promotional item is by conventional offset or letterpress printing methods. Several hundred pieces can be produced in two colors for about $25.

RADIO AND TELEVISION

Publicity may be obtained on radio in much the same way as in the newspaper. (Use the same press release.) In addition, various public-service announcements and showcase spots can be arranged.

Announcement of 10- 20- and 60-second speaking time (about 130 words per minute) can be written and supplied to the local radio stations. Make sure to hit them all—AM, FM, TV, both educational and commercial stations. If certain disc jockeys have a practice of plugging local events, make sure they receive special copy addressed to their personal attention.

Women's shows and interview programs may offer a chance to have principal players do a number from the show, or to be interviewed about all the excitement of the musical production. Local talent programs might have small audiences, but the exposure won't hurt if the stature of the program doesn't tend to brand the musical production as amateurish.

Contact the *program director* of any broadcast station to determine what details can be worked out. While speaking with him, request to have musical selections from your show programmed in regularly scheduled music shows. Usually this is the least they will do. Such cooperation builds atmosphere for the promotion effort and has recognition value when the audience sits in judgment during the performance. It's been said that a person never really gets the feel of a musical number until he has heard it three times. Certain great songs may be exceptions, but advance air play can certainly make the whole show seem more familiar.

NEWSPAPER

Through publicity, newspapers offer the most valuable means of informing and reminding the public of a coming musical. Unfortunately it doesn't pay to reciprocate because paid advertising doesn't work very well. One-time ads usually sell only a handful of tickets. A series of paid advertisements necessary to produce best results are beyond budget limits in almost every case. And then, why spend the money when better results can be obtained for free?

However, if a group is convinced that local newspaper advertising has value, or if it is available at an unusually low rate for public-service groups, care should be taken to produce an interesting ad in the same manner as outlined in the section on poster design. Simple block-letter, type-set ads say "amateur." An attractive ad conveys the idea that the production is a revival of a portion of musical theatre history.

PERSONAL APPEARANCES

A certain amount of glamour surrounds *anyone* who appears on a stage. It takes skill and a certain amount of guts. The potential ticket buyer spectrum likes to see a sneak preview and become more familiar with the show. A lot

Get Tickets Now

for the

U.D. Player's

production of

a new musical about an old operetta

J.F.K. LITTLE THEATRE

FEB. 12, 13, 14, & 19, 20, 21.

All Seats Reserved

CALL 461-5500 EXT. 281

(Figure 10-8)   Flyer used for University of Dayton production of Little Mary Sunshine *on all classroom and hallway bulletin boards.*

of people are quite surprised that a local group can achieve a polished performance—and will buy tickets. Of course, it goes without saying that you can't afford a bad performance.

Personal appearances at parent-teacher meetings, school hangouts, dances, variety shows, business group meetings, or parades, song fests, stunts, impromptu struts down main street, etc., all have promotional value and may result in further publicity. This is the very heart of "theatrical engineering" and can be a lot of fun for nonprofessionals. However, it can't be stressed strongly enough that such promotion efforts must never be allowed to *become the show* or detrimental to the primary objective, a successful musical production.

THAT "NICE" FEELING

A musical production is a terriffic amount of work. Naturally, any group wants as many people as possible to see their show. Yet, so few groups really sell their shows. People will never know they are any good unless you tell them they are. When they come you want to provide a fine evening in the theatre. Your budget, tickets, program, and promotion are an integral part of getting the audience in, entertaining them with a well-produced show, and interesting them enough to come back again. When you manage these things, *everyone* will have that "nice" feeling of having done a fine musical and an audience that appreciated it, too.

CHAPTER XI Recap

"Curtain"

If there is any sure prescription for a successful musical production, it would have to be careful selection, preplanning, proper communication between production staff members, and hard work. It also helps if you have talented people in the cast, a great orchestra, and a "cracker-jack" production crew, but there's no substitute for competent direction and leadership.

When the people on top are on the ball, the feeling and drive speeds the infectious spirit of show business momentum. Everybody wants to take part. And so they do—operating like the proverbial well-oiled machine. If you don't like the word machine, you probably prefer the word genius. If so, forget musical theatre, because no one genius or small group of geniuses can successfully bring off a full-size musical comedy. It takes a full crew of 70 to 100 people contributing their time, effort, and cooperation.

In effect, during the course of the production, your group must: form a corporation; select and educate management; hire 30 to 50 workers for onstage training; choose a construction and systems operation team; assemble 20 to 30 musicians; construct what amounts to several buildings; electrically wire and program more lighting equipment than is normally found in a square block of houses; make or rent enough costumes to clothe the football, basketball, baseball, and track teams combined; move an average of two truckloads of furniture and props, and so on—all in a matter of a few weeks.

Then when you do undertake such a venture, it's important that you do the job right, for the sake of the audience and for the profit of a good reputation for following productions. Receptive audiences and good season ticketholders aren't built overnight. One bad production can spoil the merits of several good ones.

The way different groups go about doing a musical is more than just a difference in creativity. With no formal precedent, every group has had to make do on their own. Despite this fact, returns of the Musical Comedy Production Questionnaire showed that certain patterns and trends have developed.

For those interested, this survey was sent to 276 high schools, colleges, and little theatre groups. A total of 152 questionnaires, or 55 percent, were returned. Eight were eliminated for being less than three-quarters completed. Twelve more were eliminated because they had only done one musical. The 133 groups that remained are tabulated in the following section. (Totals vary slightly due to multiple response or an occasional skipped question.)

SAMPLE QUESTIONNAIRE

Dear Sir:

As a producer or director of nonprofessional productions of Broadway musicals, I request your cooperation in compiling a complete production guide on this subject.

In my opinion, the complexities that arise with the word "musical" have never been practically presented in any single useful form. The few available books on the subject, written by professional Broadway people, offer many helpful suggestions, but miss the target on many basic principles—practices used to solve problems in a $350,000 production, for example, are not always practical in nonprofessional productions, which often have budgets of less than $1,000.

I have worked in the high-school, college, and little theatre field for over ten years and have shared many of your headaches. It has been my experience that any sizable group is capable of presenting an enjoyable musical with a high degree of professionalism. The secret lies in the preplanning and the methods in which each stage of the production is handled.

Talented people (and some not so talented) are eager to perform—and to be taught. My aim is to provide a source of guidelines and ideas that might assist other producers and directors in their productions.

This questionnaire is being mailed to a cross-section of schools and theatre groups all across the country. It is designed to test the logic of my methods and, hopefully, to produce other ideas that should be included in my book. Please complete it at your earliest possible convenience and return to me in the enclosed envelope.

Thank you very much.

T. E. Tumbusch

ALL QUESTIONS REFER TO NONPROFESSIONAL REVIVALS OF BROADWAY MUSICAL COMEDIES (NOT LOCAL REVUES OR VARIETY SHOWS)

1. We choose our musicals from: (check)

    catalogs _____   personal experience _____
    cast albums _____   recommendations _____
    other (explain) _____

2. About _____% of our musical shows meet expenses or make a profit.

3. We have/have not (circle) had to cancel any musical productions because of troubles that came up during rehearsals.

4. We have/have not (circle) ever given a bad show because it was just too much for our group to handle.

5. We once had to cancel a scheduled show because _____

    _____

6. Other than the normal production staff (director, choreographer, set designer, wardrobe mistress, stage manager, lighting and stage crew, and prop man) we find it helpful to have (*list any others*) _____

7. Our director is: (check) an experienced member of our staff _____; a professional _____; just an interested party _____; a student _____; other (explain) _____

8. One/more than one (circle) person is responsible for directing the book or dialogue part of our shows.

9. Our choreographer is: (check) an experienced member of our staff _____; a local dance teacher _____; just an interested party _____; a student _____; we don't use one _____; other (explain) _____

10. Our musical director is: (check) a school music teacher _____; a professional musician _____; just an interested party _____; a student _____; other (explain) _____

11. We use (check) full orchestra _____; pianos only _____; other (explain) _____

12. Our orchestra usually rehearses about _____ hours prior to joining the cast (underline stage of production where orchestra is *first* used) run-throughs, a week to ten days prior to opening night, dress rehearsal, other (explain) _____

13. We _____ do/do not _____ cast from outside our school or group.

14. We _____ do/do not _____ rent any scenery or drops.

15. Our sets are usually _____ realistic/impressionistic. (circle)

16. We use (type of materials) _____

    _____ to construct our sets.

17. We rent _____% of our costumes. Others are: (check) made and retained by individuals _____; made and retained by the group _____; usually available in our costume collection _____; other (explain) _____

18. We _____ do/do not _____ rent lighting equipment.

19. We _____ do/do not _____ sell a souvenir program.

20. Our productions usually run for _____.

21. Our productions are presented in: (check) a little theatre _____; an auditorium of more than 800 seats _____; in-the-round _____; other _____

    _____

22. Our facilities were built in _____. (Approx. year)

23. We _____ own/rent our facilities.

24. We have done the following musicals in the last five years: _____

    _____

    _____

25. The most successful musical we ever presented was _____.

COMMENTS I THINK WOULD BE HELPFUL IN COMPILING YOUR BOOK ARE:

_____

_____

_____

_____

_____

_____

_____

NAME _____ORGANIZATION OR SCHOOL _____

ADDRESS _____CITY _____STATE _____

SUMMARY OF ANSWERS RECEIVED

1. Where people go to find the musicals they do: (multiple response)

    112 to personal experience
     71 to catalogs
     64 ask for recommendations from groups or friends
     35 to cast albums
      2 make selection from a quantity of perusal copies
      1 from a student committee that finds a show they would like to do

2. Percent of musicals that make a profit or meet expenses:

    109—100 percent
      6— 90 "
      2— 80 "
      4— 75 "
      2— 60 "
      9— 50 "   or less (two did not charge admission)

3, 4, 5. "The show must go on" seemed to hold true for non-pros as well as legit. Only six cancellations—all acts of God—all performed at a later date, at the worst a week's delay.

6. Other titles, other than musical and choral directors, that I inadvertently left out were:

Conductor	Student Manager	Technical Director
Producer	Hair Stylist	Dressing Room Supervisor
Business Manager	Pro Seamstress	Head Usher
Rehearsal Pianist	Program Designer	Ticket Manager
Audio Man	Ad Manager	Rehearsal Conductor
Publicity Chairman	Accountant	

7. Director is usually:

    116—regular member of staff with other duties
     13—a paid professional with no other duties
      4—unpaid interested party
      1—student (assistant)

8. Seventeen groups entertain the folly of more than one director on the same show.

9. Choreographer is usually:

    64—local dance teacher (some paid—some not)
    38—member of school staff
    19—student
    11—interested party
     5—professional dancer
     4—didn't use one

10. Musical Directors are usually:

    105—school music teachers
     21—pro-musicians (some paid—some not)
      3—private voice teachers
      2—interested parties (one physics teacher)

11. Accompaniment by:

    105—full orchestras   (one school used orchestra for scene changes and dance
     17—piano and rhythm   numbers only—pianos only the rest of the time.)
     14—piano only
      1—wind group

12. Rehearsals of musicians:

    44—more than 20 hours
     1—18 hours
     2—16 hours
    16—15 hours
     4—12 hours
    13—10 hours
     7— 8 hours
    25— 7 hours or less

    Musicians join the rest of the cast:

    77—a week to ten days prior to opening night
    21—dress rehearsal only
    20—early in run-throughs

13. Cast outside group:

    53—yes (often in case of all-boy or all-girl school)
    79—no (one exception for orchestra)

14. Rent scenery:

     30—yes (mostly drops)
    100—no

15. Type of scenery used most often:

    67—realistic
    27—impressionistic
    38—both, depending on show

16. Interesting comments on set materials used:

pre-fab sets	wallpaper	upson board
plastics	war surplus materials	tobacco cloth
cut-out legs	Masonite	aluminum frames
large portable murals	burlap	ribbons

    (Among others used in text material for Chapter VII.)

17. Percent of costumes rented:

7—100 percent	8—30 percent
6— 90 "	9—20 "
3— 80 "	15—10 "
3— 70 "	10— 5 "
21— 50 "	49— 0 "
1— 40 "	

    Where do they come from? (multiple response)

    83—made and retained by group
    35—made and retained by individuals
    35—usually available in costume collection
    12—anywhere they can get them

18. Rent lighting equipment:

     27—yes
    103—no

19. Do you sell a souvenir program?

     18—yes
    109—no

20. How many performances:

    32—3 performances
    28—4   ”
    18—2   ”
    15—10 or more
    15—5 performances
     8—6   ”
     7—2 weekends
     6—8 performances
     4—9   ”

BIBLIOGRAPHY

BOOKS

Billboard's Little Theater Handbook, The. New York: The Billboard Publishing Co., 1924.

Engel, Lehman. *American Musical Theatre, The.* New York: CBS Records, 1967.

Engel, Lehman. *Planning and Producing the Musical Show.* New York: Crown, 1957. Revised 1966.

Century Theatre Lighting. New York: Century Lighting Co., 1967. (Catalog)

Dress Through the Ages. Philadelphia: Brooks-Van Horn Costume Company.

Ewen, David. *Complete Book of the American Musical Theater.* New York: Holt, Rinehart and Winston, 1959. Revised 1964.

Green, Stanley. *World of Musical Comedy, The.* Cranbury, New Jersey: A. S. Barnes and Company, 1960. Revised 1969.

Liszt, Rudolph G. *Last Word in Make-up, The.* New York: Dramatists Play Service, 1949. Revised 1959.

Report on Amateur Instrumental Music in the United States 1967. Chicago: American Music Conference, 1968.

Rockefeller Panel Report. *Performing Arts: Problems and Prospects, The.* New York: McGraw-Hill Book Company, 1965.

Simon's Directory of Theatrical Materials, Services and Information. New York: Package Publicity Service, 1963.

Spencer, Peter A. *Let's Do A Musical.* London: Studio Vista, 1968.

Smith, Cecil. *Musical Comedy in America.* New York: Theatre Art Books, 1950.

Turfery, Cossar, and King, Palmer. *Musical Production—A Complete Guide for Amateurs, The.* London: Sir Isaac Pitman & Sons, Ltd., 1953.

PERIODICALS

"Broadway: The Insides Speak Out . . ." *Playbill.* New York: Playbill, Inc., December, 1964.

Dusenbury, Delwin B. "American Musical Theater—To 1920" *Dramatics Magazine,* Cincinnati: The National Thespian Society, October 1957—May 1968. (Available in reprint booklet.)

Dusenbury, Delwin B. "American Musical Theater Since 1920" *Dramatics Magazine.* Cincinnati: The National Thespian Society, October 1958—May, 1959. (Available in reprint booklet.)

Ensley, Robert W. "Staging Musicals" *Dramatics Magazine.* Cincinnati: The National Thespian Society, October 1963—May 1964. (Available in reprint booklet.)

"Lincoln Center Does It." *Business Week.* New York: McGraw-Hill Publications, January 29, 1966, p. 36.

New York Times. New York: The New York Times Company, January 31, 1965, p. 1, Business Section.

APPENDIX

MUSICALS: WHEN THEY OPENED

In Chapter II it was explained that the opening date and age of a musical indicates a lot about writing and production styles. For that reason the following list has been compiled for use in the selection process. Also for general interest, it includes the more important musicals from the time of THE BLACK CROOK through 1942 and a complete list of musicals and major revues from 1943 through the 1968–69 theatrical season. Important off-Broadway musicals are also included and indicated with an (OB): musicals still running as of April 27, 1969 are marked with an *. In judging the number of performances it should be noted that 200 performances was considered a smash hit in the early part of this century whereas a show of the sixties must run over the 1,000 mark to merit equal status.

OPENING DATE	MUSICAL	NO. OF PERFORMANCES
September 12, 1866	THE BLACK CROOK	474
March 10, 1868	HUMPTY DUMPTY	483
July 27, 1874	EVANGELINE	Undetermined
September 4, 1884	ADONIS	603
November 13, 1903	BABES IN TOYLAND	192
November 7, 1904	LITTLE JOHNNY JONES	52
December 25, 1905	45 MINUTES FROM BROADWAY	90
December 25, 1905	MLLE. MODISTE	202
October 24, 1906	THE RED MILL	274
November 17, 1910	NAUGHTY MARIETTA	136
September 8, 1913	SWEETHEARTS	136
December 8, 1914	WATCH YOUR STEP	175
December 25, 1914	HELLO BROADWAY	123
August 16, 1917	MAY TIME	492
August 28, 1917	LEAVE IT TO JANE	167
December 21, 1920	SALLY	570
September 29, 1921	BLOSSOM TIME	592
February 7, 1923	WILDFLOWER	477
September 2, 1924	ROSE-MARIE	557
December 1, 1924	LADY BE GOOD!	330
December 2, 1924	THE STUDENT PRINCE IN HEIDELBERG	608
September 16, 1925	NO, NO, NANETTE	321
September 21, 1925	THE VAGABOND KING	511
September 22, 1925	SUNNY	517
December 8, 1925	THE COCOANUTS	377
November 8, 1926	OH, KAY!	256
November 30, 1926	THE DESERT SONG	471
February 2, 1927	RIO RITA	494
September 6, 1927	GOOD NEWS	551
April 25, 1927	HIT THE DECK	352
November 3, 1927	A CONNECTICUT YANKEE	418
November 22, 1927	FUNNY FACE	244
December 27, 1927	SHOW BOAT	572
November 27, 1929	FIFTY MILLION FRENCHMEN	254
January 14, 1930	STRIKE UP THE BAND	191
October 14, 1930	GIRL CRAZY	272
June 3, 1931	THE BAND WAGON (REVUE)	260
December 31, 1931	OF THEE I SING	441

November 29, 1932	THE GAY DIVORCE	248
April 13, 1933	THE THREEPENNY OPERA	12
September 30, 1933	AS THOUSANDS CHEER	
	(REVUE)	400
October 21, 1933	LET 'EM EAT CAKE	90
November 19, 1933	ROBERTA	295
September 22, 1934	THE GREAT WALTZ	298
November 21, 1934	ANYTHING GOES	420
October 10, 1935	PORGY AND BESS	124
November 16, 1935	JUMBO	233
April 11, 1936	ON YOUR TOES	315
October 29, 1936	RED, HOT AND BLUE	183
April 14, 1937	BABES IN ARMS	289
June 16, 1937	THE CRADLE WILL ROCK	108
November 2, 1937	I'D RATHER BE RIGHT	290
May 11, 1938	I MARRIED AN ANGEL	338
September 22, 1938	HELLZAPOPPIN' (REVUE)	1404
November 23, 1938	THE BOYS FROM SYRACUSE	235
November 27, 1939	PINS AND NEEDLES	
	(REVUE)	1108
December 6, 1939	DU BARRY WAS A LADY	408
May 28, 1940	LOUISIANA PURCHASE	444
October 25, 1940	CABIN IN THE SKY	156
October 30, 1940	PANAMA HATTIE	501
December 25, 1940	PAL JOEY	374
January 23, 1941	LADY IN THE DARK	388
October 1, 1941	LET'S FACE IT!	547
October 29, 1941	BEST FOOT FORWARD	326
June 2, 1942	BY JUPITER	427
July 4, 1942	THIS IS THE ARMY	113
January 7, 1943	SOMETHING FOR THE BOYS	422
March 31, 1943	OKLAHOMA!	2202
April 1, 1943	ZIEGFELD FOLLIES (REVUE)	554
June 17, 1943	EARLY TO BED	382
September 9, 1943	MY DEAR PUBLIC (REVUE)	45
September 16, 1943	BRIGHT LIGHTS OF 1944	
	(REVUE)	4
October 7, 1943	ONE TOUCH OF VENUS	567
November 5, 1943	ARTISTS AND MODELS	
	(REVUE)	28
November 11, 1943	WHAT'S UP	63
November 17, 1943	A CONNECTICUT YANKEE	418
December 2, 1943	CARMEN JONES	502
January 13, 1944	JACKPOT	69
January 28, 1944	MEXICAN HAYRIDE	481
April 8, 1944	FOLLOW THE GIRLS	882
April 20, 1944	ALLAH BE PRAISED	20
April 24, 1944	HELEN GOES TO TROY	64
May 18, 1944	DREAM WITH MUSIC	
	(REVUE)	28
August 21, 1944	SONG OF NORWAY	860
October 5, 1944	BLOOMER GIRL	653
November 16, 1944	SADIE THOMPSON	60
December 7, 1944	THE SEVEN LIVELY ARTS	
	(REVUE)	183
December 23, 1944	LAFFING ROOM ONLY	
	(REVUE)	232
December 27, 1944	SING OUT SWEET LAND	102

December 28, 1944	ON THE TOWN	462
January 10, 1945	A LADY SAYS YES	87
January 27, 1945	UP IN CENTRAL PARK	504
March 22, 1945	THE FIREBRAND OF FLORENCE	43
April 19, 1945	CAROUSEL	890
May 24, 1945	MEMPHIS BOUND	36
May 31, 1945	HOLLYWOOD PINAFORE	52
July 18, 1945	MARINKA	165
September 6, 1945	MR. STRAUSS GOES TO BOSTON	12
September 27, 1945	CARIB SONG	36
October 6, 1945	POLONAISE	113
October 16, 1945	THE RED MILL (REVIVAL)	531
November 9, 1945	THE GIRL FROM NANTUCKET	12
November 10, 1945	ARE YOU WITH IT?	264
November 22, 1945	THE DAY BEFORE SPRING	167
December 21, 1945	BILLION DOLLAR BABY	219
January 5, 1946	SHOW BOAT (REVIVAL)	418
January 21, 1946	NELLIE BLY	16
February 6, 1946	LUTE SONG	142
February 13, 1946	THE DUCHESS MISBEHAVES	5
March 7, 1946	THREE TO MAKE READY (REVUE)	327
March 30, 1946	ST. LOUIS WOMAN	113
April 18, 1946	CALL ME MISTER (REVUE)	734
May 16, 1946	ANNIE GET YOUR GUN	1147
May 31, 1946	AROUND THE WORLD IN EIGHTY DAYS	74
October 31, 1946	HAPPY BIRTHDAY	563
November 4, 1946	PARK AVENUE	72
December 5, 1946	IF THE SHOE FITS	21
December 26, 1946	BEGGAR'S HOLIDAY	108
December 26, 1946	TOPLITZKY OF NOTRE DAME	60
January 9, 1947	STREET SCENE	148
January 10, 1947	FINIAN'S RAINBOW	725
March 13, 1947	BRIGADOON	581
April 3, 1947	BAREFOOT BOY WITH CHEEK	108
May 1, 1947	THE MEDIUM AND THE TELEPHONE (OPERAS)	211
June 2, 1947	LOUISIANA LADY	4
October 2, 1947	MUSIC IN MY HEART	124
October 3, 1947	UNDER THE COUNTER	27
October 9, 1947	HIGH BUTTON SHOES	727
October 10, 1947	ALLEGRO	315
December 5, 1947	CARIBBEAN CARNIVAL (REVUE)	11
December 11, 1947	ANGEL IN THE WINGS (REVUE)	308
December 26, 1947	THE CRADLE WILL ROCK (REVUE)	34
January 15, 1948	MAKE MINE MANHATTAN (REVUE)	429
January 29, 1948	LOOK MA, I'M DANCIN'	188
April 30, 1948	INSIDE, U.S.A. (REVUE)	339

May 5, 1948	HOLD IT!	46
May 6, 1948	SALLY (REVIVAL)	36
June 3, 1948	SMALL WONDER (REVUE)	134
September 15, 1948	SLEEPY HOLLOW	12
September 16, 1948	HEAVEN ON EARTH	12
September 20, 1948	MAGDALENA	88
October 7, 1948	LOVE LIFE	252
October 11, 1948	WHERE'S CHARLEY?	792
October 19, 1948	MY ROMANCE	95
November 13, 1948	AS THE GIRLS GO	420
December 16, 1948	LEND AN EAR (REVUE)	460
December 29, 1948	THE RAPE OF LUCRETIA	23
December 30, 1948	KISS ME, KATE	1077
January 13, 1949	ALONG FIFTH AVENUE (REVUE)	180
January 22, 1949	ALL FOR LOVE	121
April 7, 1949	SOUTH PACIFIC	1925
July 15, 1949	MISS LIBERTY	308
October 13, 1949	TOUCH AND GO (REVUE)	176
October 30, 1949	LOST IN THE STARS	281
October 31, 1949	REGINA	56
November 25, 1949	TEXAS, LI'L DARLIN'	293
December 8, 1949	GENTLEMEN PREFER BLONDES	740
January 6, 1950	HAPPY AS LARRY	3
January 17, 1950	ALIVE AND KICKING (REVUE)	46
January 20, 1950	DANCE ME A SONG (REVUE)	35
February 2, 1950	ARMS AND THE GIRL	134
March 15, 1950	THE CONSUL	269
March 23, 1950	GREAT TO BE ALIVE	52
April 27, 1950	TICKETS PLEASE (REVUE)	245
May 18, 1950	THE LIAR	12
June 28, 1950	MICHAEL TODD'S PEEP SHOW (REVUE)	278
September 27, 1950	PARDON OUR FRENCH (REVUE)	100
October 12, 1950	CALL ME MADAM	644
November 24, 1950	GUYS AND DOLLS	1200
December 14, 1950	BLESS YOU ALL (REVUE)	84
December 21, 1950	OUT OF THIS WORLD	157
February 6, 1951	JOTHAM VALLEY	31
March 15, 1951	THE GREEN PASTURES (REVIVAL)	44
March 29, 1951	THE KING AND I	1246
April 18, 1951	MAKE A WISH	102
April 19, 1951	A TREE GROWS IN BROOKLYN	267
May 14, 1951	FLAHOOLEY	40
June 14, 1951	COURTIN' TIME	37
June 21, 1951	SEVENTEEN	180
July 19, 1951	TWO ON THE AISLE (REVUE)	276
October 8, 1951	MUSIC IN THE AIR (REVIVAL)	56
November 1, 1951	TOP BANANA	356
November 12, 1951	PAINT YOUR WAGON	289

March 21, 1952	THREE WISHES FOR JAMIE	94
May 5, 1952	OF THEE I SING (REVIVAL)	72
May 16, 1952	NEW FACES OF '52	
	(REVUE)	365
June 25, 1952	WISH YOU WERE HERE	598
October 14, 1952	BUTTRIO SQUARE	7
October 27, 1952	MY DARLIN' AIDA	89
December 15, 1952	TWO'S COMPANY (REVUE)	90
February 11, 1953	HAZEL FLAGG	190
February 18, 1953	MAGGIE	5
February 25, 1953	WONDERFUL TOWN	559
March 10, 1953	PORGY AND BESS	
	(REVIVAL)	559
May 7, 1953	CAN-CAN	892
May 28, 1953	ME AND JULIET	358
September 8, 1953	CARNIVAL IN FLANDERS	6
December 3, 1953	KISMET	583
December 10, 1953	JOHN MURRAY ANDERSON'S	
	ALMANAC (REVUE)	221
March 5, 1954	THE GIRL IN PINK TIGHTS	115
March 10, 1954	THE THREEPENNY OPERA	
	(REVIVAL) (OB)	2611
April 8, 1954	BY THE BEAUTIFUL SEA	270
April 20, 1954	THE GOLDEN APPLE	125
May 13, 1954	THE PAJAMA GAME	1063
September 30, 1954	THE BOY FRIEND	485
October 11, 1954	ON YOUR TOES (REVIVAL)	64
October 20, 1954	PETER PAN	149
November 4, 1954	FANNY	888
November 29, 1954	SANDHOG	48
December 1, 1954	MRS. PATTERSON	102
December 2, 1954	HIT THE TRAIL	4
December 27, 1954	THE SAINT OF BLEECKER	
	STREET	92
December 30, 1954	HOUSE OF FLOWERS	165
January 27, 1955	PLAIN AND FANCY	461
February 24, 1955	SILK STOCKINGS	478
April 6, 1955	THREE FOR TONIGHT	85
April 18, 1955	ANKLES AWEIGH	176
April 23, 1955	PHOENIX '55 (OB)	97
May 5, 1955	DAMN YANKEES	1022
May 26, 1955	SEVENTH HEAVEN	44
June 20, 1955	ALMOST CRAZY (REVUE)	16
September 6, 1955	CATCH A STAR	23
November 10, 1955	THE VAMP	60
November 30, 1955	PIPE DREAM	246
March 15, 1956	MY FAIR LADY	2717
March 22, 1956	MR. WONDERFUL	383
May 3, 1956	THE MOST HAPPY FELLA	678
June 13, 1956	SHANGRI-LA	21
June 14, 1956	NEW FACES OF '56 (REVUE)	220
June 18, 1956	BY HEX (OB)	40
November 9, 1956	THAT GIRL AT THE BIJOU	
	(REVUE)	11
November 15, 1956	LI'L ABNER	693
November 26, 1956	CRANKS (REVUE)	40
November 29, 1956	BELLS ARE RINGING	925
December 1, 1956	CANDIDE	73

December 6, 1956	HAPPY HUNTING	408
March 1, 1957	ZIEGFELD FOLLIES (REVUE)	123
April 13, 1957	SHINBONE ALLEY	49
April 27, 1957	LIVIN' THE LIFE	25
May 14, 1957	NEW GIRL IN TOWN	432
May 21, 1957	SIMPLY HEAVENLY	62
September 27, 1957	WEST SIDE STORY	732
October 17, 1957	COPPER AND BRASS	36
October 31, 1957	JAMAICA	557
November 6, 1957	RUMPLE	45
December 19, 1957	THE MUSIC MAN	1375
January 23, 1958	THE BODY BEAUTIFUL	60
February 4, 1958	OH, CAPTAIN!	192
February 21, 1958	PORTOFINO	3
April 3, 1958	SAY, DARLING	332
October 11, 1958	GOLDILOCKS	161
November 5, 1958	MARIA GOLOVIN	5
November 10, 1958	SALAD DAYS (OB)	80
November 11, 1958	LA PLUME DE MA TANTE (REVUE)	835
December 1, 1958	FLOWER DRUM SONG	602
December 22, 1958	WHOOP-UP	56
February 5, 1959	REDHEAD	455
March 9, 1959	JUNO	16
March 19, 1959	FIRST IMPRESSIONS	84
April 23, 1959	DESTRY RIDES AGAIN	473
May 11, 1959	ONCE UPON A MATTRESS	470
May 12, 1959	THE NERVOUS SET	23
May 21, 1959	GYPSY	702
August 4, 1959	BILLY BARNS REVUE	87
October 7, 1959	HAPPY TOWN	5
October 8, 1959	A DROP OF A HAT	215
October 22, 1959	TAKE ME ALONG	448
November 2, 1959	THE GIRLS AGAINST THE BOYS (REVUE)	16
November 16, 1959	THE SOUND OF MUSIC	1443
November 18, 1959	LITTLE MARY SUNSHINE (OB)	1143
November 23, 1959	FIORELLO!	796
December 7, 1959	SARATOGA	80
January 20, 1960	PARADE (OB)	95
February 10, 1960	BEG, BORROW OR STEAL	5
February 26, 1960	A THURBER CARNIVAL (REVUE)	127
March 8, 1960	GREENWILLOW	95
April 14, 1960	BYE BYE BIRDIE	608
April 20, 1960	FROM A TO Z (REVUE)	21
April 28, 1960	CHRISTINE	12
May 3, 1960	THE FANTASTICKS (OB)	*
May 4, 1960	ERNEST IN LOVE (OB)	103
September 12, 1960	VINTAGE '60 (REVUE)	8
September 29, 1960	IRMA LA DOUCE	527
October 17, 1960	TENDERLOIN	216
November 3, 1960	THE UNSINKABLE MOLLY BROWN	553
December 3, 1960	CAMELOT	873
December 15, 1960	WILDCAT	168
December 26, 1960	DO RE MI	400

January 12, 1961	SHOW GIRL (REVUE)	100
January 16, 1961	CONQUERING HERO	7
March 2, 1961	THIRTEEN DAUGHTERS	28
April 3, 1961	THE HAPPIEST GIRL IN THE WORLD	97
April 13, 1961	CARNIVAL	719
May 18, 1961	DONNYBROOK	68
September 26, 1961	FROM THE SECOND CITY	87
October 3, 1961	SAIL AWAY	167
October 10, 1961	MILK AND HONEY	543
October 12, 1961	LET IT RIDE	68
October 14, 1961	HOW TO SUCCEED IN BUSINESS WITHOUT REALLY TRYING	1417
October 23, 1961	KWAMINA	32
November 3, 1961	KEAN	92
November 10, 1961	ALL IN LOVE (OB)	141
November 19, 1961	THE GAY LIFE	113
December 26, 1961	SUBWAYS ARE FOR SLEEPING	205
January 27, 1962	A FAMILY AFFAIR	65
February 1, 1962	NEW FACES OF '62 (REVUE)	28
March 15, 1962	NO STRINGS	580
March 19, 1962	ALL AMERICAN	86
March 22, 1962	I CAN GET IT FOR YOU WHOLESALE	300
May 8, 1962	A FUNNY THING HAPPENED ON THE WAY TO THE FORUM	966
May 15, 1962	ANYTHING GOES (REVIVAL) (OB)	239
May 19, 1962	BRAVO GIOVANNI	76
October 3, 1962	STOP THE WORLD—I WANT TO GET OFF	555
October 20, 1962	MR. PRESIDENT	265
October 27, 1962	BEYOND THE FRINGE (REVUE)	667
November 10, 1962	NOWHERE TO GO BUT UP	9
November 17, 1962	LITTLE ME	257
December 12, 1962	RIVERWIND (OB)	443
January 6, 1963	OLIVER	775
March 18, 1963	TOVARICH	264
April 15, 1963	SOPHIE	8
April 19, 1963	HOT SPOT	43
April 23, 1963	SHE LOVES ME	302
May 16, 1963	THE BEAST IN ME (REVUE)	4
September 30, 1963	STUDENT GYPSY OR THE PRINCE OF LIEDERKRANS	16
October 3, 1963	HERE'S LOVE	339
October 17, 1963	JENNIE	82
October 24, 1963	110 IN THE SHADE	331
December 8, 1963	THE GIRL WHO CAME TO SUPPER	112
January 16, 1964	HELLO DOLLY!	*
February 6, 1964	RUGANTINO	28
February 16, 1964	FOXY	72
February 27, 1964	WHAT MAKES SAMMY RUN?	533
March 26, 1964	FUNNY GIRL	1301

April 4, 1964	ANYONE CAN WHISTLE	9
April 7, 1964	HIGH SPIRITS	376
April 17, 1964	CAFE CROWN	3
May 26, 1964	FADE OUT—FADE IN	272
September 22, 1964	FIDDLER ON THE ROOF	*
September 30, 1964	OH WHAT A LOVELY WAR	126
October 20, 1964	GOLDEN BOY	569
October 27, 1964	BEN FRANKLIN IN PARIS	215
November 10, 1964	SOMETHING MORE	15
November 21, 1964	ZIZI (REVUE)	49
November 23, 1964	BAJOUR	232
December 15, 1964	I HAD A BALL	200
February 6, 1965	KELLY	1
February 16, 1965	BAKER STREET	313
March 18, 1965	DO I HEAR A WALTZ?	220
April 25, 1965	HALF A SIXPENCE	511
May 11, 1965	FLORA THE RED MENACE	87
May 16, 1965	THE ROAR OF THE GREASE-PAINT THE SMELL OF THE CROWD	232
October 4, 1965	PICKWICK	56
October 10, 1965	DRAT! THE CAT!	8
October 17, 1965	ON A CLEAR DAY YOU CAN SEE FOREVER	280
October 23, 1965	SKYSCRAPER	248
November 22, 1965	MAN OF LA MANCHA	*
November 29, 1965	ANYA	16
December 10, 1965	THE YEARLING	3
December 14, 1965	LA GROSSE VALISE (REVUE)	7
January 25, 1966	SWEET CHARITY	608
March 7, 1966	WAIT A MINIM (REVUE)	16
March 18, 1966	POUSEE CAFE	3
March 29, 1966	IT'S A BIRD, IT'S A PLANE, IT'S SUPERMAN	75
May 17, 1966	A TIME FOR SINGING	41
May 24, 1966	MAME	*
October 18, 1966	THE APPLE TREE	463
November 20, 1966	CABARET	*
November 26, 1966	WALKING HAPPY	161
December 5, 1966	A JOYFUL NOISE	12
December 15, 1966	I DO! I DO!	584
March 3, 1967	YOU'RE A GOOD MAN CHARLIE BROWN (OB)	*
March 28, 1967	SHERRY	72
April 11, 1967	ILLYA DARLING	320
April 26, 1967	HALLELUJAH, BABY!	293
October 23, 1967	HENRY, SWEET HENRY	80
December 7, 1967	HOW NOW DOW JONES	201
January 13, 1968	YOUR OWN THING (OB)	*
January 18, 1968	THE HAPPY TIME	286
January 27, 1968	DARLING OF THE DAY	31
February 4, 1968	GOLDEN RAINBOW	385
March 3, 1968	HERE'S WHERE I BELONG	1
April 4, 1968	EDUCATION OF HYMAN KAPLAN	28
April 10, 1968	GEORGE M	427
April 23, 1968	I'M SOLOMON	7

April 29, 1968	HAIR	*
May 2, 1968	NEW FACES OF '68	34
October 20, 1968	HER FIRST ROMAN	17
October 23, 1968	MAGGIE FLYNN	82
November 17, 1968	ZORBA	*
December 1, 1968	PROMISES, PROMISES	*
December 20, 1968	DAMES AT SEA (OB)	*
January 2, 1969	FIG LEAVES ARE FALLING	4
January 22, 1969	CELEBRATION	*
January 26, 1969	RED, WHITE, AND MADDOX	41
February 3, 1969	CANTERBURY TALES	121
February 6, 1969	DEAR WORLD	*
March 16, 1969	COME SUMMER	7
March 18, 1969	1776	*
March 22, 1969	BILLY	1